TABLE OF CONTEN

Top 20 Test Taking Tips

1. Carefully follow all the test registration procedures
2. Know the test directions, duration, topics, question types, how many questions
3. Setup a flexible study schedule at least 3-4 weeks before test day
4. Study during the time of day you are most alert, relaxed, and stress free
5. Maximize your learning style; visual learner use visual study aids, auditory learner use auditory study aids
6. Focus on your weakest knowledge base
7. Find a study partner to review with and help clarify questions
8. Practice, practice, practice
9. Get a good night's sleep; don't try to cram the night before the test
10. Eat a well balanced meal
11. Know the exact physical location of the testing site; drive the route to the site prior to test day
12. Bring a set of ear plugs; the testing center could be noisy
13. Wear comfortable, loose fitting, layered clothing to the testing center; prepare for it to be either cold or hot during the test
14. Bring at least 2 current forms of ID to the testing center
15. Arrive to the test early; be prepared to wait and be patient
16. Eliminate the obviously wrong answer choices, then guess the first remaining choice
17. Pace yourself; don't rush, but keep working and move on if you get stuck
18. Maintain a positive attitude even if the test is going poorly
19. Keep your first answer unless you are positive it is wrong
20. Check your work, don't make a careless mistake

Theoretical and Knowledge Bases of Reading

Language learning and cultural context

While much attention is often given to the various cognitive and affective processes taking place inside of the learner, the cultural factors outside of the learner have just as much to do with the process of learning language. The culture within which the individual is learning determines what he or she learns, and affects when and how s/he learns it. The particular cultural setting in which someone learns, and what social interactions are participated in by the learner, have a considerable influence on what content a student learns and in what manner it is learned. Therefore, the quality of learning results is shaped not only by the student's internal process, but just as much by the student's interactions with external things and people. Various cultural institutions teach concepts valued by one's culture: children learn them at home; schools teach additional concepts; sports and arts activities teach them; and the media also contribute many cultural ideas.

Evidence of cultural influences on learning

The ways that people within a culture communicate and interact with one another and how they conduct social transactions provide evidence of the knowledge their culture has imparted to them. For example, our knowledge about how to spell words in the English language; how to use bank accounts; and what we understand scientifically about the world are taught by and show values and conventions of our cultural context. In all cultures, language represents a primary area of knowledge. Even cultures without written language use spoken or signed language, plus body language and certain social conventions to follow. One example is categorization. We categorize under the concept "BIRD," such qualities as having feathers and laying eggs. We also learn to include birds that swim; those that fly/do not fly; those that quack or sing; very small/very large birds, etc. We exclude fish, frogs, or snakes even though they also lay eggs. Without the "BIRD" concept in our culture, all members might not include all types within that category.

Culturally determined knowledge

While we may not often consider it, the meanings we assign to words are culturally determined knowledge, which we utilize to develop concepts that shape how we think. For example, a dairy farmer looking at a herd of cows differentiates breeds such as Holstein, Guernsey, Angus, Jersey, etc.; moreover, s/he observes things such as how much milk each cow gives and whether it is typical for its breed, age, and time since calving. But someone outside the dairy farming culture, such as a stockbroker, will look at the same herd and only see cows. Thus, culturally determined knowledge affects how we relate concepts: knowing names for different varieties influences us to learn and recognize their characteristics; without this information, we may not notice variations. All cultures have a language or symbol system to represent concepts. For example, in our culture, symbols we recognize only through social agreement about their meaning include Einstein's relativity formula $E=mc^2$; the McDonald's logo; or the common abbreviation of "bike" for "bicycle." Culture largely influences our perceptions.

Learning meanings assigned to symbols

In our culture, most of us are familiar with the picture of the arm and hand that means "stop" from street crossing signals and non-electronic signs, and from the manual gesture we use, where it originated. This gesture and its likeness have no intrinsic meaning that is obvious from seeing them; we have agreed socially that they mean "stop." Actions are the earliest symbols that children learn. They progress developmentally; for example, a child first reaches for a desirable/interesting object. If adults see and respond to this as pointing, the child eventually learns to point as a symbol or sign. The pointing action connects the object—an environmental stimulus, and the child's goal—to obtain the object. The child-adult social interaction imbues the child's reaching action with an additional, shared meaning of pointing. Due to this social interaction, the child then internalizes the meaning of pointing and utilizes the pointing action as a gesture; this makes the action intrapersonal as well as interpersonal.

Symbols we use that children learn

The types of symbols/signs children learn can be classified by their relation to what they represent. For example, drawings of animals, people, buildings, cars, etc., are iconic symbols—representational images of them. Indexical signs do not literally represent people/things in the environment, but rather indicate causal relationships, as with the needle on a car's fuel gauge and how far the vehicle can go. In a culture's language, words and numbers are abstract: not literal representations or relational indices, their relationship with the concepts they stand for are abstract. Such abstract, language-based symbols enable us to use higher-order cognitive skills, such as executive function. Our cultures determine procedural knowledge, like subtracting one 2-digit number from another: one might subtract the 10's column first, then the 1's; or rename the top number first; or borrow from the 10's for the 1's. Culture teaches students which procedures it values. Culture influences attitudinal knowledge by differentially valuing various attitudes; for example, cautions about being "politically correct" can clash with ethnic "profiling" in anti-terrorism initiatives.

Ways in which cultural and social influences teach us how to think

To engage successfully in our culture's social activities, we must learn the way our particular cultural and social group typically thinks. Some learning theorists, such as Vygotsky in his sociocultural learning theory, believe that we learn ways to think through our social interactions, especially when trying to solve problems that are socially defined. Vygotsky found that cognitive development entails converting social interactions into mental processes. Once we internalize these processes, we can apply them independently of other people. We initially learn our culture's ways of thought through social/collaborative problem-solving, using tools—both actions, and actual real-world objects. As Vygotsky and social learning theorists such as Bandura proposed, we learn problem-solving actions by observing and then imitating others' modeling. Physical actions can then be internalized, becoming mental actions. Our language reflects this: using cameras to save what we saw is reflected in telling people to "take a mental snapshot." Using ice to save food is reflected in the expression about putting an idea "on ice" to save it for later.

Inner speech

Babies and young children typically learn spoken language through hearing people in their environment speaking it. Adults having experience with toddlers are familiar with hearing them "talking to themselves" or "thinking aloud" when they are working through a cognitive task: verbalizing their thoughts helps them to "talk themselves through" the reasoning and steps required. Vygotsky proposed that this "private speech" eventually becomes internalized, so that the child can do it mentally rather than audibly. Inner speech, which is a type of thought, is evidence that the child has internalized language. It enables higher-order thinking. It enables children and adults to plan operations before performing them. It also facilitates approaching and solving problems without being bound by their specific context, because it allows learners to think beyond their immediate environments. They can approach dissimilar situations and those not in the present time or place. They can organize their behavior at multiple complexity levels, and generate action plans.

Children's literacy development

Infants begin literacy development when they hear language spoken to and around them. They become aware of speech as a medium of communication. Soon, they are also exposed to children's books and begin to develop print awareness, including discriminating between speech and print. This first stage of literacy development is known as the stage of awareness and exploration. Parents can support this stage by reading aloud to babies from board books with bright colors and large, simple images. Reading them poems, including nursery rhymes, also helps as their repetition attracts infants' attention. Babies learn by exploring their environment; toddlers, with their increased locomotion, expand their exploration. Parents can help them learn language by associating environmental objects with their word names. Pointing to things and asking "What's that?" is an effective game for learning vocabulary. In this stage, children also develop letter recognition and association of letters with the phonemes (speech sounds) that they represent.

From the first stage of literacy development in which babies and toddlers develop awareness and exploration of spoken and printed language, they become preschool children and move into the stage of experimental reading and writing. During this time, children are typically learning to sing the "Alphabet Song," whereby they memorize every letter in the alphabet. They are learning to associate certain letters and the sounds that they represent with words most significant in their lives, such as the spelling of their names and their parents' names, and the numbers and words in their home addresses. At this age, preschool children are typically very interested in looking at books. Parents can take advantage of this natural motivation by continuing to read aloud to their children every day, and also encouraging them to read words out of the books themselves. At this stage, children are also likely to start scribbling, producing written letters and numbers, and write their own names. Parents can provide challenges by pointing at signs outdoors and having children name their letters.

Babies and toddlers first develop awareness and exploration of spoken and printed language; preschoolers develop experimental reading and writing skills. Once they begin kindergarten and first grade, children are in the early learning reading and writing stage; these skills are further developed by formal schooling. In school, children typically learn phonics, i.e., recognizing the speech sounds (phonemes) associated with letters and being able to combine two or more phonemes and letters to create words. Because their orientation is primarily phonetic or sound-oriented rather than orthographic or spelling-oriented at this point, it is common and normal for children to spell phonetically rather than according to orthographic conventions. For example, many children will write "pikcher" to represent the sounds of the word spelled "picture." Additional developments during this stage include children now understanding that printed words are separated from other words by spaces; and that they understand the concept of sentences constructed from words.

The first stage of literacy development is awareness and exploration of spoken and written language; the second involves experimenting with reading and writing; and the third focuses on the early learning of reading and writing in the formal education setting. The fourth stage is considered one of transitional reading and writing, typically during the second and third grades of elementary school. Children can not only associate printed words and sentences with spoken language; moreover, they can now also recognize the meanings of printed words and can read on their own. In this stage, they are starting to gain an understanding of the significance of written language, and their reading comprehension improves. At this time, children typically can read a statement and comprehend its main thesis. They can combine multiple ideas to understand the overall "big picture." Parents and teachers can help children better comprehend the books they read independently, by suggesting that they relate the stories to their own lives.

Babies and toddlers (stage 1) develop awareness of spoken and written language and explore its uses in their environments. Preschoolers (stage 2) experiment with early reading and writing, and children entering formal school settings (stage 3) learn further literacy skills. By the fourth stage of transitional literacy, second and third graders gain greater reading comprehension and begin to read independently. The fifth stage is considered that of competent reading and writing, which typically develops by fourth grade and thereafter. By this time, children are skilled enough at reading that they can learn and comprehend new or unfamiliar words, including those that are complex. They are able to read long novels rather than just short stories. They can comprehend the meanings and themes in the reading without adult help. As children become older, they may develop more or less interest in reading; however, their reading skills are maintained from this stage onward. Adults can encourage children's continued motivation to read by providing them with books on subjects that individually interest them.

Creating effective literacy learning environments

Young children need print-rich learning environments that facilitate and enhance their phonological awareness and supply them with ongoing reinforcement of direct instruction. Teachers should provide young children with continual, ready access to books and other literary materials, rather than simply storing them on shelves. They should expose young children to many varieties of print. A classroom library containing both fiction and non-fiction books should be located centrally, and include newspapers, magazines, telephone books, restaurant menus, etc. Teachers should also integrate literacy across the curriculum by reading and assigning texts that support their learning units in subjects such as mathematics, sciences, and social studies. For example, they can teach sequencing during science experiments by using graphic organizers. They can visually display the relevant number words and math terms during classroom calculations so the children can see these math processes represented phonetically as they work with them.

- 8 -

Stimulating literacy development

In addition to providing continual, easy exposure and access to reading and writing materials, continually reinforcing their direct instruction, and integrating literacy across the subject content curriculum, teachers should also choose literacy materials according to children's abilities and needs. They should include texts for various reading levels in their classroom libraries to allow all children to experience reading success. They can supply concrete objects, such as picture cards of alphabet letters and plastic letter manipulatives, which help beginning readers to decode printed words. They can borrow more sophisticated books from teachers of higher grades to provide challenges for more advanced young readers. Teachers' daily reading aloud to classes affords their participation and motivation. Teachers can model expression by varying their voices to represent various characters in fables and fairy tales. Informal 30-minute reading periods twice weekly, in which children and teachers all read silently for pleasure, also enhance motivation. Technology can support literacy development; for example, teachers and students can use digital dry-erase whiteboards for instruction in phonics, vocabulary, and text structure.

Primary differences and similarities among listening, speaking, reading, and writing

One major similarity between listening and reading is that they involve receptive language; and a main similarity between speaking and writing is that they both involve expressive language. These characteristics also represent the major difference between receptive listening and reading vs. expressive speaking and writing. While there is overlap, different areas of the brain process these two sides of language. Because one must first comprehend language in order to produce understandable linguistic output, receptive language develops sooner than expressive language. Therefore, children are hearing and beginning to understand spoken language that they hear before they begin to speak; and after listening to books read aloud to them, they begin to read before they begin to write. Deficits in listening comprehension can delay speech development, and deficits in reading ability will also be reflected in the products of writing attempts. Listening and reading require decoding sounds and letters/words, an analytic process; speaking and writing require encoding these, a synthetic process: the latter depends on the former.

Physical, situational, and structural differences between spoken and written language

The simplest, most obvious difference is that speech is produced by the vocal organs, and writing, by the hands. Though both involve the brain, some of the structures, functions, and processes involved differ too. Speech is received auditorily, and writing, visually. Beyond physicality, spoken and written communications are used in different situations; consequently, as communicative methods they are related but independent. For example, people prefer speech when within earshot of each other. They write when distance or time prevents speaking. Historically, written documents have been respected as more permanent and legally binding than oral accounts, which undergo more changes through repeated transmissions. Today, archived sound recordings are starting to mitigate this difference. Written vs. spoken vocabulary and grammar differ. Vocal variations in speech convey meanings that cannot be written, and vice versa. For example, Allies in World Wars vs. general "allies" are better differentiated in writing than speech. "She's suntanned all over" means her *visible* body, while whispering the "all over" means *all* parts; this cannot be written.

Fundamental contrast separating speech and writing; how they are related; and an area of writing where they come together

When we study speech, we are studying the sounds we produce and hear for communication. When we study writing, we are studying the visual symbols we produce and see for communication. Yet in language, these two separate modalities are related: people (except in Deaf culture) learn to read and write through relating visual symbols to speech sounds. For correct spelling, the two modalities of speech and writing must come together. However, it is inaccurate to regard writing, as many people do, as simply speech put in writing: rules are stricter for writing than for speech, and speech incorporates vocal cues to meaning that writing cannot. However, many people also judge speech according to writing, which is also inaccurate. For example, many written words contain "silent" letters not voiced, and many words are spelled differently from how they sound. Moreover, despite the importance of speech for social interactions, our society places value on the standards set by our written language, as well as its global provenance and more lasting nature.

Aspects of contrast between speaking and writing

Speaking is more dynamic but also more transient and time-sensitive than writing, which is more static but also more enduring. Speech is governed by time, and writing, by space. Speakers usually know to whom they are speaking, but writers often do not know who will read what they write. Spoken conversations are too fast and spontaneous to plan them in advance in any complex way; conversely, writing can be planned, organized, edited to be more concise, reread repeatedly, and analyzed. Written layout and punctuation makes discourse units such as sentences and paragraphs easy to recognize, while these boundaries are frequently less obvious in speech. Speech includes more rewording/rephrasing, and repeating, looser grammatical constructions, and sentence fragments, etc., as it cannot be edited as writing can. Speech includes more comment clauses, such as "you know," for the same reason. Because of visual cues like gestures and facial expressions used in spoken communication, speech is typically vaguer, using directions such as, "right now," "in here," and "that one," which have to be further explained in writing.

General examples of how spoken and written language differ

Two major differences between spoken and written language are that when we write, we do not receive immediate feedback from our audience as we would when speaking; and that we cannot depend on our immediate context to establish the meaning of our writing as we can in speech. Therefore, while we can use deictic (i.e., directly pointing out) expressions in speech, such as "that one right there," or "all of us," and the meaning is made clear by the setting and/or visual indicators such as physical gestures and facial expressions, in writing these become too ambiguous and are usually avoided. Writing is also subject to the effects of time passing before it is read, and to varying interpretations by diverse readers; these are both necessary for writers to consider, whereas (live) speech has more immediacy and is more likely to be interpreted with less variation by listeners within the same context.

Features of speech that are not represented well in writing

When people speak, a salient aspect of their speech is prosody. Prosody also exists in, and is studied in, written poetry, but not as much in other writing. Prosody is made up of a number of components, such as vocal intonation, pitch, tempo (speed), loudness, rhythm, tone of voice, and other vocal characteristics that the speaker varies to indicate meaning, including not only semantic distinctions but also expressions of emotions, attitudes, and other information not contained within the words themselves. Most of the elements of prosody constitute unique features of speech. It is quite difficult to represent these features efficiently in writing. In writing, unique features not found in speech include: capitalized words; punctuation marks more related to grammatical rules than to indicating spoken features*; spatial organization; lines of writing/print; and pages. *Some written conventions related to spoken prosody include: question marks; italics, underlining, and boldface for emphasis; commas and semicolons indicating pauses rather than/in addition to grammatical divisions; and periods indicating ends of thoughts, as well as grammatically of sentences.

Examples in which speech and writing are used in combination rather than as distinct media

Normally, we speak for a listener to receive our message immediately. However, when we leave a voice mail message for someone over the phone, we expect it to be received later. We may even speak with the intention of not being heard, as with *sotto voce* comments or talking to ourselves. When we produce speech that we expect to be put into writing, such as dictating a letter, we speak more carefully and correctly than in conversation and direct the transcriber to ignore any spoken errors and dysfluencies. In other speech that we expect to be written down, such as giving a police statement or a legal deposition, we tend to speak more naturally as the listener has the job of recording it. Some activities depend on writing and speech mutually. For example, a teacher conducting a lesson or a public speaker giving a presentation may be writing on an overhead projector and simultaneously, talking. In these situations, neither video nor audio recording alone would capture the full presentation.

One way in which technology has altered the characteristics of spoken and written communication

Before the advent of electronic communications, speech was typically an interactive process. However, once telephone answering machines and then voice mail had been developed, speech could be not just a dialogue as usual: people are required to produce monologues when leaving spoken messages, which will not be heard until later, so that speech in this category is not immediately interactive in the same way. Conversely, writing historically has not been immediately interactive due to the passage of time between when the writer produces the written communication and when the reader actually receives it. However, since technological advances have created e-mail, instant messaging, text messaging, and online chat windows, these time constraints have been drastically decreased or eliminated, so that people's written (typed) communications occur in real time, often as quickly as they would in spoken conversations—even among distant parts of the world. Thus in this aspect, writing has been rendered interactive, more similar to speech.

Phonemic awareness

Phonemic awareness consists of being able to hear, identify, and manipulate individual speech sounds or phonemes. The manipulation of speech sounds includes such processes as breaking words down to individual components; blending phonemes and words; and stretching them. For children to read printed language, they must first develop phonemic awareness. This enables their understanding that words are composed of phonemes, which are the smallest units of sound in a spoken word that affect its meaning. For example, changing the phoneme /s/ to /m/ changes the word *sat* to *mat*, a different word and meaning. Children can demonstrate phonemic awareness by identifying words in a group that start with the same phoneme, such as *book, boy,* and *bicycle*. They can isolate and pronounce the initial or final phoneme in a word, such as /d/ or /g/ in *dog*. They can blend phonemes to say a word, e.g. "/d/, /o/, /g/--*dog*." They can conversely segment words into phonemes, e.g. "*dog*--/d/, /o/, /g/."

Alphabetic principle

The alphabetic principle is the concept that letters represent speech sounds, and arrangements of letters represent spoken words. When children learn the predictable, systematic relationships of letters to sounds, they can apply their knowledge of these relationships both to words they know and to new words. This enables them to develop reading fluency. Children's treating words as series of letters and remembering written word forms correlate highly with their knowing the shapes and names of letters. Children seem to acquire alphabetic knowledge in this sequence: first, they learn letter names, by singing the alphabet song and reciting alphabetic rhymes; then, they learn letter shapes, by playing with 3-dimensional wood or plastic letters, lettered blocks, and alphabetic books; and then, they learn letter sounds as they relate the letters they see to the speech sounds that they hear and produce. Instruction in phonics assists children in learning and applying the alphabetic principle by explicitly relating visible written letters to audible spoken sounds.

To help young children understand the relationship between speech sounds and written letters, i.e., the alphabetic principle, teachers should instruct them in letter-sound correspondences in isolation, one pair at a time, and teach these directly and explicitly. Teachers should also integrate in their daily lessons, in all subjects, plenty of opportunities for children to practice the letter-sound relationships they have been explicitly teaching in isolation. Teachers should both review cumulatively all the letter-sound correspondences they have already taught with children, and introduce new sound-letter relationships into both their isolated, direct, explicit lessons and into the opportunities they provide them with for practicing. Early in their instruction and frequently, teachers should give young children ample opportunities for applications of their growing repertoires of sound-letter correspondences by providing them with words whose meanings are familiar to the children, and spelling these phonetically.

Teachers should base their instructional rates on the group performance of their class. While there is no set rule about order of introduction, educators agree that letter-sound relationships with the highest utility—meaning they help children start reading words as soon as possible—should be taught first. For example, the letters *a, s, m, t,* and *p* have high utility in our language, while *gh* in *through, x* in *box, a* in *want,* and *ey* in *they* have lower utility and can be taught later. Consonants that are continuous, such as /s/, /f/, /m/, /n/,

- 12 -

and /r/, are easier for children to produce in isolation than stops such as /b/, /p/, /g/, /k/, /d/, /t/; and continuous consonants that are initial or medial in words are easier for children to blend than stops in these positions. Visually confusing letters such as /b/ and /p/ or /p/ and /g/, and auditorily confusing sounds such as /b/ and /v/ or /i/ and /e/, should be taught separately. Instruction should match children's learning rates.

According to research, more teacher-directed, explicit instructional methods are more effective than indirect and implicit techniques. Many teachers combine various instructional methods. Teachers should keep in mind that individual children vary in the rates at which they learn sound-to-letter correspondences. Educators find a reasonable rate for introducing new sound-to-letter relationships to be between two and four pairs per week. Consonants and vowels should be introduced in an order that allows children to read words as quickly as possible. The earliest relationships teachers that should introduce are those between the letters and sounds that are used the most in the language. When introducing consonant letters and sounds, teachers should separate single consonant sounds from consonant clusters and blends by putting these in different lessons. They should not introduce letters that look similar and/or sounds that sound similar at the same time. And they should give instruction in blending using words containing letter-sound correspondences that the children have already learned.

Phonological processing

During listening and speech vs. during reading and spelling
When we are listening to speech and/or speaking, our phonological processing is largely unconscious. The primary task of listening is to comprehend the meaning of speech, and that of speaking is to convey comprehensible meaning, for communicative purposes rather than to focus on the speech sounds produced; so phonological processing is automatic. In contrast, reading and spelling written language involve more metalinguistic processes (i.e., thinking about and understanding how we use language); these do not come naturally and are not learned easily. However, phonological skills are not highly correlated with intelligence. Some individuals with high cognitive abilities have deficits in phonological awareness. The correlation between phonological awareness and learning to read and write, though, is much stronger in any alphabetically-based written language, and also in non-alphabetic written languages, such as Chinese and Japanese, which are ideographic.

Phonemic awareness

Children cannot decipher our writing/printing system, its patterns, or its representation of spoken language without phonemic awareness. For example, if you ask a child who has not developed good phonemic awareness to tell you the first sound in the word *dog*, they may say "Bow-wow!" Until they can identify the phoneme /d/ in *dog, good,* and *Dad,* and isolate it from these words' other sounds, children cannot understand what the letter *d* stands for in the words. Research consistently finds that we can predict quite accurately whether children will later read well or poorly, even before they learn to read, by testing their awareness of phonemes in words, their knowledge of letter names, their knowledge of sound-to-letter correspondences, and their vocabulary. Research also finds that the majority—at least 80%—of poor readers also show weak phonological awareness and/or phonological memory; and poor spelling is associated with phonological processing deficits. Studies also find that direct, explicit instruction in phonemic awareness remediates reading and spelling problems and speeds alphabetic learning.

Phonological awareness

When students pay attention to words that they do not know, their phonological awareness and their memories are activated as they compare the unfamiliar/new words to words that they already know, which helps them to comprehend and pronounce the new ones. When they hear a new word, their ability to repeat it and pronounce it correctly also depends upon their phonological awareness and their memories. When students hear or read new words, they must be able to encode them correctly in order to remember them; in turn, they must be able to remember them to retrieve them and use them appropriately in their speech and writing. In addition, when students hear words that are similar in sound, they must be able to differentiate between or among them in order to determine their respective meanings. Without good phonological awareness and memory, students are more apt to confuse words that have completely different meanings if they are similar in sound.

American elementary school-aged children's reading proficiency

A substantial proportion of American children have been found not to read well. For example, the National Assessment of Educational Progress (NAEP) defines the "basic" level of reading proficiency as "...partial mastery of the prerequisite knowledge and skills that are fundamental for proficient work at each grade" (2009). The NAEP's 2009 Reading Report Card found that 33% of fourth-graders in America read below this "basic" level. Many beginning kindergarteners are below grade level and/or behind their peers, and continue to be behind in successive grades. Variations in children's personal, familial, cultural, and socioeconomic backgrounds, life experiences, and exposure to print differentially affect their reading abilities, especially as upper school grades present more challenging reading matter. Research identifies these differences by ages of 3 years. Students with sufficient prior knowledge attain good reading comprehension, while those without it do not. The NAEP finds that proportionally more impoverished, black, and Hispanic students score below "basic" levels on its reading test than their age peers.

Learning to read

Presence or absence strongly predicts how easily they will learn to read
Children are predicted to learn to read well in first grade when, as preschoolers, they have developed: (1) recognition of the letters of the alphabet, and the ability to name them; (2) general print knowledge, such as recognizing the front and the back of a book and knowing how to turn its pages; and (3) phonemic awareness, i.e., recognizing, differentiating and manipulating the individual speech sounds/phonemes in words. Giving younger children exposure, experience, information, guidance, and practice with reading builds these three skills. Therefore, parents should read aloud to their babies from birth onward, and read aloud together with them as they develop the abilities to repeat what parents read, to identify letters in words, and to associate some letters with certain speech sounds. Reading aloud with children is the most important activity parents can do to prepare their preschoolers to read. Indeed, many children begin learning to read through this activity before they enter school.

Aspects of social interaction that influence how children learn to read
The ways that parents communicate with their young children influence how the children learn to listen and speak, which contains many of the skills necessary to reading and is

strongly correlated with their learning to read. For example, when parents and caregivers sing rhyming songs and play word games with young children, they are developing the children's phonemic awareness. When a very young child just learning to speak has heard and recognizes the word "cookie" and knows what it means and when s/he attempts to produce it and says "cook," her parent responds, "Do you want a cookie?" This helps the child construct knowledge of meaning; reasons for communicating; vocabulary; syntax; and sentence structure. This knowledge will support the child's later reading skills. Early identification of and intervention for hearing, speech, and/or language deficits in young children are crucial for preventing future reading problems.

Finding reading problems early

While many children can read by first grade regardless of instruction methods, those who cannot require help to catch up: studies find the majority (88%) of those with reading problems at the end of first grade still have them at the end of fourth grade; and ¾ of third-graders who read poorly still read poorly in high school. These findings show how important it is for parents, caregivers, and teachers to establish sound foundations for reading to children from their birth through 5 years of age. Research has shown that most children who read poorly (85-90%) can attain average levels of reading skills through prevention and early intervention programs that integrate instruction in phonemic awareness and phonics, spelling, reading fluency and comprehension, delivered by well-trained teachers. Of children with reading disabilities, up to 2/3 are found to be able to read at average or above-average levels with early identification and effective instruction. Helping children learn to read is a responsibility shared among parents, caregivers, community members and programs, and teachers.

Social learning theory

Pioneered by psychologist Albert Bandura, social learning theory proposes that we learn largely through observing the actions of others and then imitating them. Bandura also first discovered that children did not need to engage in an action themselves to learn from it: they could observe another child receiving rewards for doing something and realize the connection between behavior and consequences. Bandura calls this vicarious learning. He found children will then imitate actions they observed to obtain the same rewards. When parents read to their young children, they are not only exposing them to new vocabulary, rules of sentence arrangement and grammatical patterns; they are moreover modeling reading behaviors for children to imitate. When parents point out specific letters and help children sound them out, they are teaching phonemic awareness and the alphabetic principle. As they learn these, children also eventually imitate parental models and begin to read letter sounds and words. Too, the pleasure of closeness and interacting with parents reinforces (rewards) the reading activity.

Piaget's theory of cognitive development

Piaget's cognitive-developmental theory is among those considered constructivist. Constructivism, broadly summarized, is the view that we (humans) are active learners and construct our own meaning from the reality we experience. Piaget proposed that children move through different stages of cognitive development, through which their understanding and reasoning abilities progress to enable higher levels of thinking. These levels correspond closely to the emerging skills they demonstrate, and to their ages of enrollment in preschools, nursery schools, kindergarten, and elementary grades and what they are taught there. For instance, children are unlikely to comprehend most abstract concepts much before middle school ages, and they need concrete objects to observe and manipulate to perform mental operations until they do. Piaget also stated that children are like "little scientists" exploring, investigating, and interacting with their environments to learn and actively construct meaning. All people with whom they come in contact are parts of their environments, so their social interactions with people are included as interactions with their environments.

Fluency and non-fluent reading

Reading fluency is an ability to read printed text with speed, accuracy, and (when reading aloud) appropriate expression. Fluent readers automatically recognize the words in a text when they read it silently. To derive meaning from what they are reading, they use strategies such as quickly grouping words into phrases, clauses, and sentences. When fluent readers read text out loud, they do so without effort, and they use natural-sounding vocal expression the same way as when they are speaking spontaneously. Non-fluent readers, in contrast, read slowly and laboriously, one word at a time. When reading aloud, they sound choppy rather than smooth. Fluent readers decode words effortlessly and automatically, identifying and understanding words simultaneously—freeing their attention to focus on the meaning. They form connections among the concepts presented in the text, and between these and their prior knowledge. Readers less fluent divert too much attention to decoding words, so they have little left to focus on understanding the meaning.

Students develop reading fluency gradually, through much practice and time. The oral reading of students whose reading development is in the earliest stage is slow and effortful because they are first learning how to associate letters with sounds and to blend the letter sounds into identifiable words. When students achieve the ability to identify many words automatically, their reading aloud is still not fluent if they read without expression. In order to incorporate expression, readers need the ability to divide the text into "chunks" of meaningful information. They also need to know when to pause during and between sentences, which words to emphasize, and when to change vocal tones. For example, as the Partnership for Reading points out, a fluent reader will read this line from *Brown Bear, Brown Bear* by Bill Martin Jr. with appropriate pauses and intonation: "Brown bear/Brown bear/What do you see?" while a non-fluent reader will read it, likely in a monotone voice, with misplaced pauses: "Brown/bear brown/bear what/do/you see."

The three levels of reading fluency are the Frustration, Instructional, and Independent levels. At the Frustration level, the text is hard for the student to read and s/he will attain lower than 90% accuracy in decoding words. At the Instructional level, the text is challenging for the reader but not frustrating, and the reader achieves 90% word accuracy. At the Independent level, the student finds the text relatively easy to read and attains 95% accuracy in recognizing and understanding its words. Fluency instruction should utilize text that the student can read at his/her Independent reading level. This is because students can focus on practicing reading speed and expression, instead of on decoding words, at their Independent levels. Fluency is not a fixed stage where readers can read all words easily and rapidly; it varies with text and subject familiarity. For example, even students who normally read very fluently may read slowly and laboriously with highly technical text on an unfamiliar subject, such as medical journal articles or nuclear physics textbooks.

Repeated and monitored oral reading

In repeated and monitored oral reading, students read and re-read text passages aloud several times, with their teacher providing feedback and guidance to correct and enhance fluency in their subsequent re-readings. This considerably improves their word recognition, reading speed, and reading accuracy along with their reading fluency. It additionally improves reading comprehension. Repeated reading is effective in elementary grades and remedially helpful for upper-grade students struggling with reading. Teachers have often traditionally used "round-robin" reading, wherein students take turns reading parts of a text, for developing oral reading fluency. However, this is not effective for fluency, because students read too small a portion of text, and because they do not read it repeatedly. Research finds that reading and re-reading orally until they reach an acceptable fluency level—typically four times for most students—is more effective. Judiciously designed feedback on reader performance during repeated readings gives the reader guidance. Using tutors, peers, audio recordings, etc., can also augment practice with reading aloud.

Silent, independent reading

Much research has revealed a strong correlation between a student's reading ability and the amount of time that the student spends reading. In fact, how much time they spend reading is considered one of the primary differences between poor and good readers. Because of these conclusions, experts have advised teachers for many years to encourage students to read voluntarily in classrooms. The literature in reading education and teacher education frequently offers classroom procedures, such as Silent Sustained Reading (SSR) and Drop Everything and Read (DEAR), to motivate students to read independently. However, research does *not* show that reading silently and independently with little or no feedback or guidance yields any improvement in reading fluency or achievement. Instead, studies find direct reading instruction to be most predictive of reading achievement. Nevertheless, teachers should not overlook the importance of providing students with time to read silently from books they can read at their Independent fluency level—i.e., they can read them with 95% word accuracy—to apply their reading skills.

Orthography

Orthography means spelling. Traditional spelling instruction concentrated on memorizing; however, research findings about orthographic layers inform moving away from memorizing to the word study approach. In word study, students learn through "word work," various hands-on activities teachers assign for exploring three layers of orthography: alphabetic, pattern, and meaning. In studying the alphabetic layer, students match letters and letter pairs (such as *sh, th, ch*) with corresponding sounds and form words from them. When studying the pattern layer, they find larger patterns in letter groupings— for example, the consonant-vowel-consonant-final *e* (CVC*e*) pattern in words such as *love, hate, more, move, fine, face,* etc. When they study the semantic layer, students come to understand how spelling reflects semantic relationships; for instance, *composition* is spelled with a medial *o* because it is derived from *compose*. Studying orthographic layers helps students understand how written words operate by enabling them to identify their derivations, patterns, and regularities; and helps them strategically apply this information for decoding new words and writing with correct spelling.

Morphology

Morphology is the study of word structure as formed from the smallest units of meaning, called morphemes. A morpheme can be as small as the letter *s*, when added to a singular noun to make it plural, such as *cat + s = cats.* Changing morphemes can change the meaning of both a word and its sentence. For instance, "Mother bake**s** cookies" means she does this in the present tense, and/or in general. Changing *-s* to *-ed* yields "Mother bak**ed** cookies," meaning she did this in the past. Letter groups like roots, prefixes and suffixes are also morphemes. For example, the words *progress, egress,* and *digress* all contain the same "gress" root from Latin *gradi*, to go, with different prefixes: *pro* meaning forward, i.e., go forward; *e* meaning out, i.e. go out or exit; and *di* (from *dis*) meaning away or aside from, i.e. to go away from the subject. Students understanding morphemes can more easily discern word meanings, and decode complex new words through recognizing their morphological parts.

Syntax

Syntax is the group of principles that determine the order of words in sentences and how they function in sentences to communicate meaning. Syntax is sometimes broadly equated with word order, but it incorporates language mechanics, sentence variation, and grammar as well. In terms of word order alone, not knowing syntactic rules affects reading comprehension and understandable as well as grammatically correct writing. Altering syntax can create meaningless sentences, as with "Street went down he the" (vs. "He went down the street"). Or it can produce completely different meanings: "She knows what to do," "She knows not what to do," and "She knows what not to do" have three distinct meanings, based simply on the presence or absence *and* position of "not." Linguist Noam Chomsky differentiated syntactic rules from word meanings/semantics by composing the famous sentence, "Colorless green ideas sleep furiously." Though grammatically correct—adjectives modify the noun subject and an adverb modifies the verb—it is meaningless. Ideas cannot be *both* green *and* colorless; furiously does not normally describe sleeping.

Semantics

Semantics refers to word meanings. Knowing more word definitions and knowing some single words have multiple meanings enhances reading comprehension and fluency. Semantic feature analysis helps students to grasp important concepts and make connections and predictions. It also improves their skills in reading comprehension and vocabulary development. This strategy shows both similarities and differences in words and emphasizes each word's uniqueness. Moreover, it activates students' previous knowledge, and it reveals information about word meanings through discussion. It is used before, during, and after reading with individual students, small groups, and whole classes. The teacher chooses a topic/category; gives the students key topic aspects and vocabulary words; and makes a chart with topic features across the top and vocabulary words down the left side. Students mark a + sign for vocabulary words fitting a topic feature and a – sign for those not fitting it; or a blank if unknown. For example, in language arts, students might compare book genres; in science, students might compare/contrast characteristics of different kinds of dinosaurs.

Semantic feature analysis

Semantic feature analysis accesses students' prior learning, teaches word meanings, enhances vocabulary and reading comprehension, and facilitates mastering essential concepts, recognizing connections, and making predictions. For example, the teacher might list names of several U.S. presidents across the top of a semantic feature analysis chart; and several salient features down the left. One such chart (Jones, 2012) lists FDR, JFK, Nixon, Reagan, and Clinton across the top; and Democrat, Wartime President, Congress of Same Party, Re-Elected, Served in Congress, and Won Majority of Popular Vote down the left. Students place a + or – in each cell of the grid—e.g., + for FDR, JFK, and Clinton and - for Nixon and Reagan with Democrat. Some cells have both + and - for the same feature, i.e., Congress of Same Party for FDR, Reagan, and Clinton; and Won Majority of Popular Vote for Nixon. This would also help students define, compare/contrast, and understand various government types, such as democracy, dictatorship, monarchy, republic, etc., by categorizing their similar and differing characteristics.

Influence of the purposes of written language

One factor that is required for children's motivation to learn to read is their understanding and appreciation of the functions and purposes of written language. They must develop awareness of the presence of printed language surrounding them in the environment—not just in books, magazines, and newspapers, but also on labels, billboards, traffic signs, street signs, directional signs, store signs, etc. Accompanying this awareness, children must realize that these various forms of print serve a great many different purposes. In reading and writing, some instructional activities that support children's understanding and appreciation of written language include: activities helping children realize that print represents spoken language; activities highlighting the uses, production, and meanings of print in classroom directions, notes, posters, calendars, labels, and signs; and activities teaching directionality and other print conventions. Other instructional activities that support children's understanding and appreciation of written language include: activities giving children practice in handling books (finding front and back covers, page tops and bottoms, turning pages); activities using patterned, predictable stories to give children practice; and word awareness lessons building knowledge of word appearances, lengths, and boundaries.

Context

The physical, social, and cultural contexts in which writers and readers operate shapes the decisions made by writers in composing their texts; and the decisions made by readers in constructing meaning from those texts as they read them. The context surrounding a writer influences, and even determines, that writer's purposes for writing what s/he does and how s/he writes it. Additionally, the choices made by writers are influenced by the limitations, opportunities, and requirements available, which themselves are influenced by the writers' contexts. Context affects readers' efforts to construct meaning from writers' work as they read it. The reader's physical context can make their ability to read a text better or worse. A reader's social context influences how many experiences and expectations, and which ones, the reader shares in common with the writer of the text s/he is reading. And cultural context influences the basic beliefs, assumptions, and desires that a writer incorporates into a text; and those that a reader brings when reading it, affecting his/her interpretation.

Genre

Texts with typical forms that share factors such as the type of author, type of consumer, topic covered, medium/media used, manner of writing, and its occasion constitute one definition of literary or writing genre. Genre is observed to delimit both the behaviors of writers and the expectations of readers, and therefore, to constitute an unspoken/unwritten agreement between them. Contemporary genre theorists find that these generic expectations serve as a kind of code or shorthand that renders written communication more efficient and economical. Though genres dictate particular conventions, authors of individual books within any genre also invent some new components. Some scholars find that when readers operate within writing genres to understand the texts they read, they are actively constructing meaning from them. The categorization that genres create serves to decrease cognitive and psychological complexity for the reader. Generic structures can make generic conventions more obvious to readers, which can highlight a text's content by differentiating between its generic form and its original content.

Application of Theoretical and Knowledge Bases of Reading in Instruction

Learning the foundations for reading

Children begin learning and experimenting with language in their earliest months. Infants' babbling emulates the vocal tones, rhythms, and expression of adult speech. Very young children start making associations between words they hear and what they represent. When they enjoy playing "peek-a-boo," "patty-cake," and similar interactive games; listening to familiar rhymes and songs; and manipulating letter blocks and board books, they are learning to employ various symbols. At the same time, they learn that print also symbolizes meanings. As they begin to understand the alphabetic principle, they cognitively process the letters they encounter, convert them to sounds, and associate the letters and sounds with meaning. While, to some observers, it can appear that some children seem to gain such understanding "magically" or independently, research is more suggestive that adults have given them much instruction and guidance, even if they do so informally and playfully. Children's early years are also characterized by diverse experiences with spoken and written language.

Linguistic experiences encountered by young children

Researchers have identified significantly diverse, linguistic experiences encountered by young children, at home, during child care, and in social situations. Studies have found that children meet with many different kinds of linguistic resources and different degrees and kinds of support for their early experiences and learning of reading and writing. While some children are provided with easy access to ample ranges of reading and writing materials, other children have less access. Some children often observe their parents reading and writing, while other children rarely or never see this. Some children are given informal, casual support, while others are given direct instruction by adults. The implication of this variety is that there is no single teaching approach or method that can be expected to be most efficacious for every child. Competent teachers instead utilize many different teaching strategies to address the diversity among children found in schools. Instruction should build on children's existing knowledge and abilities. It should also furnish children with skills, knowledge, and attitudes, and habits promoting life-long learning.

General areas about which young children need to learn

Children need to learn about the technical skills involved in reading and writing. Moreover, they need to learn how to employ these skills as tools to improve their thinking and reasoning skills. Numerous studies identify reading aloud to children as the one most important activity for developing skills and understanding required for successful reading and writing. Research has found that when children feel emotionally secure and also participate actively in reading, the result is a high quality of book reading. Teachers or caregivers working with small groups are found to enhance children's comprehension and vocabulary by asking questions requiring analysis and prediction. Children can discuss pictures in books, retell the stories read, identify their favorite parts, and often ask for

- 21 -

repeated re-readings (a typical characteristic of young children). Discussion empowers children to connect stories with their own lives. One researcher (Snow, 1991) described such discussions as, "decontextualized language," wherein teachers can stimulate higher-order cognition by helping children bridge story events from what they see, to what they can imagine.

Essential objective for adults to pursue with preschool-aged children

At preschool ages, much research supports that optimizing children's exposure to printed language and their ideas about it is an essential objective. One way teachers do this is to use Big Books to assist young children in noticing and differentiating many features of print. For example, they can help children realize that it is not the pictures, but the print, that delivers the story's meaning. They can show them how series of letters are words; that printed words represent spoken words; and that we read printed English from left to right and top to bottom. While reading stories with young children, teachers can point out specific words; guide children's attention to where the reading begins; and give children assistance in recognizing the shapes and sounds of different letters. Indeed, these ways in which teachers demonstrate how print functions have been identified by some researchers as being the keys to developing word awareness and other concepts that are crucial to children for learning to read and write.

Practice

In addition to teachers' instructional strategies and the activities they design for children to participate in with print, children additionally must be given opportunities to practice what they have learned, by themselves and with their peers. Research finds that physical classroom arrangement can support children's spending more time using books. For example, having a classroom library gives children instant access to books and other print materials. Taking children to attend the school's main library and/or a public library regularly, and helping them get library cards, assures that children can update their print collections on an ongoing basis, and may encourage them to develop the life-long habit of learning through reading. Young children are observed frequently pretending to read in comfortable library environments: they remember certain words from their favorite stories by using visual cues. This pretend reading can show children's considerable knowledge regarding the purposes of reading and its global characteristics.

Kindergarten students' acquisition of reading and writing

Many children know something about the ABCs when they start kindergarten. It is important for kindergarten teachers to build on this knowledge by helping them to gain fluency in easily identifying and differentiating among letter shapes. Research has established well that kindergarteners' letter-naming proficiency is highly predictive of their achievement at the end of the year, likely due to its mediation of memory for sounds. Learning theorists recommend beginning with the upper-case letters that are visually the easiest, and progressing to lower-case letters. They also find that mastery is facilitated, not by introducing many letters at once, but by introducing only a few at a time. Developmentally, children's ability to name letters easily coincides with their ability to associate letters with speech sounds. However, phonemic awareness also requires practice and time to develop fully. Kindergarteners with good phonemic awareness can identify rhyming and non-rhyming words, and words with the same initial or final sounds; they can segment short words into individual phonemes, and blend phonemes into words.

Assessment and instructional planning

Young children should undergo initial screening to determine their literacy levels before teachers plan their instruction. Children's literacy status and progress should also be assessed frequently and continuously, both to monitor their learning and to inform instructional planning. Long-term research into student reading development shows that the majority of third-graders evidencing weak reading skills, also had difficulty with phonological awareness and phonologically related reading skills from the time they first began school. Moreover, assessment identifies students' specific areas of weakness with the highest probabilities of causing difficulties with reading. This enables teachers to design instructional plans that target these specific weaknesses and their remediation. This targeted instruction frequently averts students' failing at reading later on in school, as well as promoting most students' reading development.

Effective reading instruction

One part of effective reading instruction involves (1) phonemic awareness, (2) knowledge of letters, and (3) print concepts. Variations in young children's early success with reading and spelling are not due as much to their intelligence, levels of maturity, or listening comprehension, as to their levels of phonemic awareness and knowledge of letter-sound correspondences. Children who are found to have poor development of phonemic awareness by the end of kindergarten are more likely to read poorly in later grades. Teachers can mitigate young children's risk of later failure in reading by giving them explicit instruction in identifying sounds, matching phonemes, segmenting words into phonemes, and blending phonemes into words, and associating sounds and their symbols. This type of explicit instruction also speeds up the early acquisition of reading and spelling for all young children.

Importance of the alphabetic principle to effective reading instruction

For children to succeed in the first and subsequent grades, they must understand sound-to-letter correspondences, as well as having phonemic awareness and letter knowledge. They must know phonics in order to identify words accurately and fluently. Overall successful reading, even at older ages, depends in large part on the ability to read words. Poor readers are likely to rely on the surrounding context to decipher new words; good readers use their decoding skills, name new words, and then, associate meaning with them. They only use context for assistance in figuring out a new word's meaning once they have decoded it. These decoding skills are also important to beginning readers for facilitating fluency and automaticity in reading. Students who read fluently (i.e. quickly and easily) are far more likely to have good reading comprehension. Therefore, providing material at the student's Independent level—i.e. s/he needs no assistance and achieves 95% word accuracy—is important. Some poor readers have learned fundamental phonics but still have specific difficulties with automatic, fluent reading.

Vocabulary and comprehension

The wider children's experience is with reading, the greater their acquisition of word knowledge, which is crucial for reading comprehension. School-aged children are required to learn thousands of new word meanings each year, the majority attained by hearing words read aloud and/or reading words in books themselves. The basis of rich, productive vocabulary is forming networks of conceptually-related words. To establish this foundation, children must actively process word meanings; this develops their comprehension of words, connections among word concepts, and word uses. Solid background knowledge and a large working vocabulary enable text comprehension. Even before children can read independently, teachers can provide instruction in comprehension through reading interactively and often with children from diverse expository and narrative texts. They should select texts that build on students' existing knowledge of the world. When teachers ask questions and invite student questions and discussions to confirm understanding, they improve students' text comprehension. Students are supported by effective instruction in relating textual concepts to their own experience/knowledge, and then retaining these ideas.

Interrelationship of children's reading and writing

Reading and writing are inextricable; some educators call them, "two sides of the same coin" (Learning First Alliance, 2000). Just as we cannot speak intelligibly without being able to listen to spoken language, we cannot write without being able to read. Reading and writing are both dependent on fluent comprehension and application of language on multiple levels. Reading and writing reciprocally benefit one another. Beginning in first grade (or sooner), children are afforded daily occasions for organizing their thoughts, transcribing, and editing them by writing. Experts recommend teachers provide writing assignments that both fit student ability levels and vary in nature. Teachers should assign both expository and narrative writing, for instance. While children are developing skills in forming letters, spelling words, and generating sentences, teachers should also teach them the stages of composition. First they can work as partners or groups to produce and organize ideas. Then they can create drafts; share ideas with peers for feedback; and, successively, learn and practice revision, editing, proofreading, and publishing.

Handwriting and spelling

Researchers have found that in the same way that fluency in recognizing words supports reading comprehension, mastery of handwriting and spelling skills supports written composition. Students who learn to form letters accurately and fluently and spell words correctly and easily write better-organized, lengthier compositions. Teachers must instruct students concurrently in composition strategies—such as identifying main ideas; writing topic sentences, introductions and conclusions; paragraphing appropriately, etc.—and in the required writing conventions, such as spelling, handwriting, capitalization, punctuation, and word usage. Explicit instruction in spelling and handwriting skills from first grade on, and frequent assignment of purposeful writing applying these skills enable students to learn them more easily. Effective teachers stimulate students' appreciation and enthusiasm for reading and writing. Research finds children read to frequently and encouraged to enjoy books and read extensively have better chances of becoming good readers. In addition to teaching specific literacy skills, selecting varied reading materials, using libraries, integrating literacy across the curriculum, and continual school initiatives promoting love of books and reading strengthen literacy instruction.

Teaching students to self-monitor their own reading comprehension

Educational researchers find that most students need explicit instruction that is intensive and given consistently, repeatedly, and over time in order to become good readers. Teachers select strategies that closely fit with the text they assign students to read. By "thinking aloud" and modeling, teachers describe and demonstrate each strategy and its importance. They guide students to learn when, where, and how to apply strategies; and they provide opportunities for students to apply them independently. After modeling, teachers guide students to practice deciding when and how to use strategies independently, giving them feedback and starting discussions. Teachers also have students independently apply the same strategies to other texts in later lessons. To enhance self-monitoring, teachers model for students how to: plan and clarify beforehand their reading's purpose/goal; consider their existing knowledge before and during reading; know whether they comprehend the text; apply strategies for deciphering hard words and concepts; question whether text makes sense; and discern how texts are organized. Teachers provide scaffolding/support that they gradually withdraw as students develop independence.

Narrative text and story grammar

Simply put, narrative is text that tells a story. This can include fables, myths, tall tales, legends, folk tales, fantasy and science fiction, short stories, novels; even some news reports, biographies, autobiographies, etc. Narrative structure usually has a beginning, middle, and end; and clear story grammar, i.e. elements of the story, including plots, themes, settings, characters; a central conflict; and a conflict resolution. Assisting students in learning to recognize recurring story grammar/elements gives them a "story schema," i.e. a mental construct of what comprises a story. With new stories, students can apply this schema to predict what could happen as the story unfolds; to imagine the looks, sounds, and behaviors of characters and settings; and summarize events in the plots. Teachers can enhance comprehension and self-monitoring by: inviting students to relate narrative characters and events to their own life experiences; focusing class discussions on story grammar; having students compare the structures of different stories they have read; and creating story maps and/or other visual aids to support recalling particular elements.

Expository text versus narrative text

Expository text is text that is factual. It provides information, rather than telling a story as narrative text does. The main purpose of exposition is to inform the reader, explain something, or persuade the reader. Some examples include academic textbooks, journals, magazines, catalogues, brochures, diaries, and generally newspapers, biographies and autobiographies (some of these latter three may use narrative structure, but many use expository form). Throughout school especially, and also throughout life, students will read mostly expository text. To comprehend exposition, students must understand how the text is organized. Exposition lacks the storyline of narrative to guide their reading. Students must learn that authors use various structures to organize their thoughts in expository writing, such as comparison and contrast, time sequences and order sequences, cause-and-effect relationships, and patterns of problems-solutions. In a given text, section, or chapter, authors can employ several or all of these structures. Exposition can also be presented differently than narrative: headings and subheadings may organize it; graphics such as diagrams, tables, charts and illustrations may be included.

Reading expository text with good comprehension

Expository text does not have a plot or storyline and characters the way that narrative text does, so students will not be focusing on those elements. Instead, they must understand the structure of exposition to comprehend what they read. Teachers can help them monitor and direct their reading of exposition independently by teaching them the following strategies: (1) to "chunk" textual information by grouping related concepts; (2) to summarize a text's most important information, also by grouping related ideas; (3) to integrate the information in an expository text with their own established knowledge; (4) to apply the information in an expository text to situations in real life; (5) to interpret the graphics, such as figures, tables, and charts in a text, and to be able to construct their own graphics; (6) to synthesize (i.e. pull together) the information from various texts that they read; and (7) to develop and deliver class presentations about the subject matter in the text they read.

Motivation

Student motivation is vital to both their reading enough and their comprehending what they read. Students' learning to read is significantly aided by motivation, as are higher student literacy levels. The broader a student's reading experiences, the greater his/her ability to understand a broadening variety of the kinds and difficulty levels of texts. Good readers read copiously, in school and independently, choosing diverse texts for various purposes, such as for information, learning, curiosity, and entertainment. To support student motivation, teachers can: give students daily opportunities to read both texts they choose and those teachers and peers recommend; frequently afford both student-led and teacher-led discussions of their reading; arrange cooperative learning groups to discuss their reading and help one another select the best strategies for each text; encourage students to read for learning about ideas and/or subjects they find meaningful; engage them actively in reading-related pursuits; encourage independent reading; and give them opportunities to select from among texts with various reading levels and genres.

Self-monitoring

As teachers, we must monitor whether students self-monitor during reading and how much: lack of self-monitoring undermines comprehension. Young children/early readers should self-monitor for 1:1 matching in beginning pattern books. They may use their fingers to help match print to sound. Early readers must monitor that the words they read look and sound right and make sense, learning to cross-check multiple information sources. All ages of students must self-monitor for punctuation cues to comprehend sentence meanings. Students must also self-monitor their pacing, phrasing, and fluency. Teachers can remind them if their reading sounds choppy to themselves, they should go back and realign elements to be smoother. Students reading longer texts self-monitor whether they are following the plot, distinguishing among characters, keeping track of settings, narrators, etc. With non-fiction, students should automatically ask themselves whether they understand it; whether the information is new to them; which parts seem more or less important; and check the context for meanings of unfamiliar (especially if bold-faced) words.

Critical thinking

When children read, their ability to think deeply about the book or its subject is a simple example of critical thinking, which takes time, experiences, and conversations to develop, and which they will need throughout life. As important as it is for adults to read to and with the youngest children, adults should also continue reading with children who can read independently. This helps children handle more challenging books with more complicated plots, more difficult vocabulary, and longer chapters and total length. Adults model and instruct patience and persistence and supply information, guidance, and support for children by working through challenging books together. To think critically, readers must slow down; adults must take time to help children reflect upon what they read. They might discuss what we learn about a character's personality from his/her actions; or the importance to the overall message of a book's setting; or a conflict in the plot. Adults can ask more open-ended questions, for which children can give many correct answers.

One instructional technique to help students apply critical thinking to reading content-area texts is the I-Chart Procedure (Hoffman, 1997). It has three stages: Planning, Interacting, and Integrating and Evaluating. Planning: students identify a topic to study from their subject-area texts. They develop questions to answer in reading. They then make a big chart for recording information they will collect, including entries of teacher and student questions; sources; the topic; what they know; other interesting information, e.g., figures and/or facts; and other questions. Gathering topic-related materials completes this stage. Interacting: students record their existing topic knowledge, plus other information they may collect. The teacher also elicits and records pertinent student questions. With teacher guidance, students read and discuss information sources. Integrating and Evaluating: students summarize each charted question, including collected information; compare summaries to background knowledge; clarify as needed; discuss what they learned; additionally research unanswered questions; and report their findings to the class. Teachers initially provide scaffolding—modeling and directing—and gradually withdraw support as students independently apply strategies.

Directed Reading and thinking Activity (DRTA)

The DRTA (Stauffer, 1975) emphasizes reading as a process of thinking. It does this through its goal of teaching students to make predictions continually as they read narrative texts. While students are reading, the teacher interrupts them at selected, strategic spots in the story and asks them to predict what they think will happen next. The teacher also asks the students to confirm, reject, or change the story purposes they identified and the predictions they made. After students are done reading, the teacher asks the students to find any part(s) of the text that support what they predicted, and to read these aloud. They also require students to use the text itself to explain their own reasoning; and to supply proof that the students' predictions were correct or incorrect. Teachers may instruct the students to use charts for recording what they predict, and corresponding information they find in the text that proves or supports the accuracy of their predictions.

K-W-L

K-W-L (Ogle, 1986) stands for Know, Want, and Learned—i.e., What I Know, What I Want to Learn, and What I Learned. These are the areas covered by each step of this procedure, which helps students learn thinking habits related to good reading—specifically, determining their purposes for reading a text, and activating their background knowledge when reading new material. In the Know step, students discuss what they already know about a topic in the text they will read. Teachers have students list topic-related concepts, and then organize their thoughts into general categories. Thus, students relate new information they read to their existing knowledge. In the Want step, students learn to establish their own purposes for reading, and in this way, also actively self-monitor their comprehension. In the Learned step, students' expressing information in their own terms improves their realizing what they do and do not know. Following these steps reinforces students' learning from reading, engages them in good reading habits, and teaches them metacognition about their own processes of reading.

Questioning the Author

Questioning the Author (Beck et al, 1997) is a procedure that stimulates students to reflect on what an author is trying to say in expository text that they read. This reflection is intended to help students create mental representations of the information they read. Teachers collaborate with students to understand the text, clarify any confusing parts, and improve comprehension. The procedure incorporates discussion, instruction in reading comprehension strategies, and self-explanation by the students. To help students realize that some parts of texts can be confusing and limit their comprehension, the teacher models questioning techniques. The class will focus on a certain portion of a text, and the teacher will ask questions, such as, "What is the author trying to say?" "Why does the author say this?" "What did the author mean by this?" etc. The teacher and students discuss what strategies they can resort to when they encounter comprehension difficulties. Students learn to tackle challenging text by imitating the teacher's questioning models.

Reciprocal Teaching

Reciprocal Teaching (Palincsar and Brown, 1984) is described as a dialogue between teacher and students, wherein each member of the dialogue responds to the other. The class or group is reading a chosen text, and the teacher-student dialogue will focus on some portion of that text. The dialogue is organized by the application of four strategies for reading comprehension: (1) asking questions; (2) clarifying challenging ideas and words; (3) summarizing the material that the students have read; and (4) predicting what might occur next. Questioning, clarifying, summarizing, and predicting are examples of critical thinking in reading. First, the teacher models application of a comprehension strategy for the students, explaining this process. The teacher gradually transfers this activity to the students. Commensurately with their growing proficiency, the teacher increases the challenge levels of student participation. This helps students to recognize the benefits of applying comprehension strategies in real-life reading activities. It also helps teachers identify individual student problems in applying these strategies, and give individualized instruction to meet student needs.

Transactional Strategy Instruction (TSI)

Transactional Strategy Instruction (Brown and Coy-Ogan, 1993) is an instructional procedure that teaches students to use effective comprehension strategies to construct meaning from the text they read. It supports students in completing the following tasks: (1) planning and setting goals for reading; (2) activating their background knowledge and using textual cues to construct meaning from the text as they read; (3) self-monitoring their reading comprehension; (4) solving problems they experience while reading; and (5) self-evaluating their progress. To achieve these, teachers using TSI instruct them in applying reading strategies, which usually include the following: making predictions based on activating their previous knowledge; generating questions and asking them; clarifying where needed; visualizing the content that they read; relating the content in the text they read to their own existing background knowledge and experience; and summarizing what they have read. TSI is practiced in small groups, using these strategies to organize discussion of text, as students read orally and exchange their individual responses to and interpretations of the reading.

Decoding and phonics

Basically, being able to apply one's knowledge of patterns in printed letters and of correspondences between letters and the sounds they represent, and to pronounce printed words correctly, constitute word decoding. When children understand letter patterns and letter-sound relationships, this affords them the capacity for quick recognition of familiar words, and for deciphering unfamiliar words. While children have been observed to arrive at a comprehension of some relationships of letters and sounds by themselves, the majority of children will become more successful at understanding these when they are also given explicit instruction in decoding. One way that educators can give such explicit teaching is through instruction in phonics. Phonics teaches children the principles that guide the relationships of letters to sounds; it teaches them the process of sounding out printed words they see; and it teaches them the exceptions to the rules that are the main guiding principles of the relationships of letters and sounds.

Children who are beginning to learn to read are apt to verbalize difficulties with decoding words using global, general terms, e.g., that reading is "stupid" and/or they "hate" reading. However, if they could articulate the problems they are experiencing more specifically to inform concerned adults, their descriptions would likely include the following factors: (1) When they try to read the words in a chapter of text, they get stuck attempting to figure out many of those words. (2) They expend so much of their energy trying to decipher the words in the text that they don't have enough left to consider the meanings of those words. (3) When they encounter unfamiliar words in a text, they do not know what to do to sound out those words. (4) They know the appearances and names of the letters in the alphabet, and they know all of our language's speech sounds; however, they are still unable to read printed words on a page.

Parents observing their children trying to read at home may notice several areas of difficulty with phonics and decoding. For example, a parent may find s/he often tells the child what many printed words say because the child cannot decipher them and gets "stuck." Parents may observe their child reading at a very slow rate because s/he takes so much time figuring out many of the words. The parents may find their child is so preoccupied with attempting to sound out words that s/he demonstrates little comprehension of the reading. Parents may realize their child does not seem to know how to read words by synthesizing the information in the reading. They may find if they try to guide their child by telling them to "sound out" words, the child's frustration only increases. In addition, parents may notice their child uses only the first one or two letters of a word to guess at it, rather than focusing on all printed letters.

Teachers may notice that a student who makes numerous spelling errors and has trouble reading also finds it difficult to match letters with the sounds they represent. Difficulty with phonics and letter-sound correspondences usually impedes reading and spelling. A teacher may observe that a student's decoding of words is very laborious. A student who finds it hard to spell or read phonetically likely has decoding and phonics deficits. When the teacher designs activities using phonics and phonetic patterns, students who have marked trouble with these are apt to have problems with decoding words and using phonics. Students who tend to hazard guesses at printed words, based only on the first letter or couple of letters, are more likely to have decoding deficiencies, so they avoid sounding out words. A teacher may find that even after s/he has taught several letter sounds or patterns, the student cannot identify these in reading, and/or the student's writing samples do not reflect these.

When parents and teachers find that some children have difficulty with phonics principles and decoding printed words, they can give them some strategies to help themselves. For example, adults can give children magnetized letters to play with, and ask them to sing the Alphabet Song while arranging the letters into alphabetical order as rapidly as they can. Adults can guide children to observe the print and writing in materials inside the household and on signs outdoors to see whether they can find letter patterns and words that they recognize. Parents and teachers can advise children to compose text messages, e-mails, written/typed notes and letters to their relatives and friends. Adults can also remind children as they write these communications to attend to each speech sound they are hearing as they write them down. Adults should also remind children to attend closely to every letter in a printed word to try to sound it out, rather than only the first one or two letters.

With young children beginning to read, parents can help them learn the alphabet letters and their corresponding speech sounds. Periodically, parents should point to letters and have children name them. Parents can help children form associations between words they see on signs and/or in newspapers, etc., and the school lessons on sounds and letters they are learning. Parents can encourage and reinforce children's using their knowledge of sounds and letters to write notes, letters, e-mails, etc. When children encounter words with irregular spellings (e.g. *was, said,* or *are*), parents should discuss these with them regularly so they learn to recognize them on sight, since they do not fit normal letter-sound rules. Parents can take advantage of computer software for developing phonics and early literacy skills, including some programs featuring writing support. For example, some software programs give children practice with short vs. long vowel sounds, and with constructing compound words; others invite children to construct sentences, which are then acted out by animated characters.

To help young children in developing early literacy skills, when teaching a specific phoneme (speech sound), teachers can give children three-dimensional objects and pictures, and have them sort these by that sound. Teachers should repeatedly have children say the letter's sound aloud every time they identify or differentiate it. To establish a solid foundation for reading and writing, teachers should use explicit and systematic instruction in phonics. If the school's curriculum materials are not designed for systematic, explicit phonics instruction, teachers should consult their reading specialists or school principals. Experts deem it best to begin this early phonics instruction by first grade. To help them comprehend the function of phonics, teachers should not only teach students phonics information, but also have students apply this learning by engaging them in reading and writing activities that demand such application. Concrete manipulatives, such as magnetized letters, counters, sound boxes, etc., help younger students learn letter-sound correspondences. Teachers can also group students based on their literacy needs, delivering more instruction where indicated.

Reading comprehension strategies

Strategies for reading comprehension do not begin as automatic or intuitive practices; they are, rather, consciously developed plans that good readers employ for understanding the text they read. These plans consist of series of steps that readers apply to make sense out of their reading. When teachers give students instruction in reading comprehension strategies, this assists the students in developing control over their own understanding of the reading and developing into active, purposeful readers. One key strategy that students can use is to develop skill at monitoring their own reading comprehension. One component of monitoring is recognizing whether one understands something one reads or not. Another monitoring component is having identified and developed strategies to address comprehension problems as they occur. Research finds that even beginner reading students can improve their self-monitoring of comprehension with instruction. With such instruction, students learn to differentiate clearly what they do and do not understand, and to apply suitable strategies to address comprehension difficulties.

Answering questions about the text they are reading can help students understand it better. Four kinds of questions are: (1) "Right There" questions exist in the text, requiring one correct answer found in one place, such as a sentence/word. For example (using Arnold Lobel's *Frog and Toad* I Can Read Books series): "Who was Frog's friend?" Answer: "Toad." (2) "Think and Search" questions require recalling information located directly in the text, usually in multiple places. Students must think about and search through the passage for the answer. For example: "Why was Frog sad?" Answer: "Because his friend left." (3) "Author and You" questions ask students to comprehend text and relate it to their prior knowledge. For example: "What do you think Frog felt, seeing Toad again?" Answer: "Happy; I'm happy to see my friend who lives far away." (4) "On Your Own" questions require students' previous experiences and knowledge more than text. For example: "How would you feel if your best friend moved away?" Answer: "Sad; I'd miss him/her."

Metacognition

Metacognition is defined as "thinking about thinking," i.e., thinking about the process of thinking itself. To attain control over their reading, good readers use metacognitive strategies. For example, they may determine their reason(s) for reading and preview their texts before they read. While they are reading, they may review whether they understand the text; resolve any comprehension challenges they encounter; and vary their reading rates according to the level of difficulty of the individual text. After reading, they check their comprehension of the text. Student strategies for self-monitoring comprehension include locating a problem; e.g., a specific paragraph and page they don't understand; identifying an author's specific sentence/statement whose meaning they don't understand; rephrasing a challenging passage or sentence using their own words to clarify its meaning; reviewing parts of the text they read earlier to inform and help themselves understand parts they are currently reading; and looking ahead for more information in the text that may explain what they are currently reading.

Graphic organizers

Graphs, charts, diagrams, maps, frames, webs, and clusters are all types of graphic organizers. They illustrate visually the concepts in a text and/or relationships among concepts. They benefit readers by helping them focus on particular ideas/concepts, and on how these are related to and interact with other ideas/concepts. Graphic organizers are tools that students can use to explore and demonstrate the relationships in a text. They can help students to focus on structural differences in texts as they read them; for example, between fictional and non-fictional writing. They also help students to compose organized summaries of text they read. Venn diagrams help students compare/contrast information from two books. Chain-of-events/storyboards help students order text events/steps in correct sequences. Story maps help students chart fictional narrative structures, e.g., identify settings, characters, events, problems, and resolutions; or identify main ideas and details as non-fictional expository structures. Cause-and-effect graphics help students visualize antecedents and consequences.

Question-Answer Relationship (QAR)

Giving students questions, and/or helping students to formulate questions, to answer when they are reading provides students with purposes for their reading. Answering questions directs students' attention to focus on what they will learn from their reading; it encourages students' active thinking while they are reading; it prompts students to self-monitor their own reading comprehension as they read; and it supports students in reviewing the information they read and relating it to their existing knowledge. The QAR strategy helps students learn to improve their ability to answer questions about their reading. QAR asks students to classify the information they use to answer questions about their reading as explicit, i.e. it is directly stated in the text; implicit, i.e. it is implied in the text; it is derived completely from their own prior knowledge; or it is some combination of these.

Generating questions, recognizing story structure, and summarizing text

When students must generate questions about what they read, they realize whether they understand it and whether they can answer their own questions. They learn to ask themselves questions requiring that they synthesize content from different portions of the text, such as questions about the text's main ideas and its important information. When students are taught to recognize content categories such as settings, characters, events, problems and resolutions in narratives, they learn to recognize story structure, frequently aided by story maps; this enhances their reading comprehension. Instruction in summarizing what they have read teaches students to discern what is important in the text they read, and to be able to express the important content in their own words. When they learn through such instruction to summarize their reading, students are better able to identify its main ideas, and to connect these; to generate central ideas from their reading; to avoid or delete superfluous information; and to remember what they have read.

Scaffolding

Scaffolded instruction, also called cognitive scaffolding/mediated scaffolding is a structured instructional method that combines serial step procedures and explicit tasks with personal support. Support is initially highly structured and intensive, gradually diminishing as students develop proficiency in following the procedures. Teachers remove multi-layered instructional supports, and then simpler support tools such as guides and prompts, little by little as students' skills grow and they become more self-directed, active learners. For example, teachers start lessons with simple concepts to which students can relate; they associate these with students' previous experiences, and/or furnish opportunities for students inexperienced with some concepts to familiarize themselves with these. Teachers then build upon these basic concepts by providing more challenging material via group and/or individual questioning, graphic aids and other supplements. Cognitive Strategy Instruction in Writing (CSIW) (Englert et al, 1991) and the Early Literacy Project (ELP) (Englert et al, 1994, 1995) are two examples of programs that use scaffolded instruction.

Cooperative learning

Cooperative (or collaborative) learning does not involve simply grouping students for assignments. It moreover requires each student to participate actively and directly in gaining knowledge by interacting and collaborating within a group of 4-6 students. Some models of cooperative learning also allow students to work in pairs. Teachers provide instruction in cooperative learning procedures, and give students opportunities to attain and practice the skills that enable successful studying skills, such as taking notes, organizing information, communicating with their peers, prioritizing, and time management/following schedules; and also enable successful group interactions. According to educational researchers (Johnson & Johnson, 1990), cooperative learning aims to develop, at a minimum, these five areas in students: (1) positive interdependence, wherein individual success depends on group success; (2) positive face-to-face interaction, such as sharing, comprehending, and developing group knowledge; (3) individual accountability; (4) small-group and interpersonal skills, such as communication, decision-making, and conflict resolution; and (5) reflection, on both the social and academic processes involved.

Studying strategies

(1) Note-taking: Teach students to use flash cards and index cards; to highlight salient text portions; to use advance organizers, which integrate existing student knowledge with targeted learning; and to use graphic organizers, which make concepts visual. Advance and graphic organizers are also tools for (2) Outlining material from lectures/lessons, and texts, and for writing essays/papers. (3) To support Summarizing skills, instruct students in the "big picture" and main ideas; use strategic integration; provide elaborative instruction; and provide advance and graphic organizers. Employ advance and graphic organizers for improving student (4) Knowledge management as well. To support student (5) Self-questioning, use the SQ3R method: Survey, Question, Read, Recite, and Review; provide elaborative instruction; and teach the Multipass (Schumaker et al, 1982) learning strategy for improving reading comprehension. To incorporate the use of (6) Adaptive materials/alternative reading materials, provide simplified texts and aural reading for students with learning/reading/other disabilities or alternative learning styles. (7) Memory aids include mnemonic devices, such as like acronyms, acrostics, and grouping by association.

Verbal rehearsal

Verbal rehearsal is a behavior we all use to maintain information in our working memory and/or short-term memory; for example, we look up a phone number, and then repeat it aloud, *sotto voce,* or silently, continually until we dial it. Students can use verbal rehearsal to learn, remember, and apply small amounts of information within a limited time period. The keyword method is a strategy of visualizing pictures that can help students learn new vocabulary and new concepts. Students construct a mental picture of anything/everything that helps them remember—an image of the thing they want to remember, an image of the printed word for it—whatever works for each student. The keyword method is one form of visualization that focuses on a key word to remember. Visualization in general is creating a visual mental picture of a concept, which could be a word, numbers, a formula, or a visual image without verbal or numerical symbols.

Metamemory

Metamemory means thinking about memory, i.e. understanding how we remember. Metamemory skills help students retain and retrieve information; through both awareness of strategies for storing and recalling, and ability to apply their repertoires of these strategies. One mnemonic device to improve memory is grouping by association. For example, it is difficult to remember a group of unrelated words, such as like *lion, China, nose, Australia, eyebrow,* and *elephant.* Teachers can prompt students to notice that two of these are animals, two countries, and two parts of the face. This both facilitates retaining the six terms, and supplies metamemory processing through pairing them by category. Acronyms are also metamemory devices, used frequently in everyday life: saying *FBI* helps us remember *Federal Bureau of Investigation,* or *CIA* for *Central Intelligence Agency.* Acrostics are myriad mnemonics creating sentences from the initials of word strings, such as, "**My Valuable Elephant May Jump Suddenly Unless Natives Prevent**," representing the solar system's order of distance from the sun: **M**ercury, **V**enus, **E**arth, **M**ars, **J**upiter, **S**aturn, **U**ranus, **N**eptune, and **P**luto.

LISTS and FIRST strategies

These two strategies' names are acrostics. They help students scan for testable items in printed/written material; categorize and group selected items; and transfer their information to index cards. **LISTS:** The student first **L**ooks for clues—finds lists of information in textbooks and class notes s/he needs to learn and heads/names each list; **I**nvestigates the items s/he found, deciding which ones to include in each list; **S**elects a mnemonic device;* **T**ransfers the information to an index card with the list and mnemonic on one side and the list name/heading on the other side; and **S**elf-tests, i.e. studies, by looking at the name/heading and using the mnemonic device to recall the list. *FIRST helps design acronyms/acrostics for mnemonics: **F**orm a word—write capitalized initials of each listed word; try forming a memorable real/nonsense word; **I**nsert lower-case letters if needed; **R**earrange the letters to form a word; **S**hape a sentence of words with the initial letters of each listed word; and **T**ry different combinations of steps to create the mnemonic.

Multipass

The Multipass Strategy (Schumaker et al, 1982) was researched with students having learning disabilities (LD) and found to improve reading comprehension by helping students glean more information from printed text. It has three main parts: the Survey pass; the Size-Up or Textual Cues pass; and the Sort-Out pass. In one step of the Survey pass, students read the chapter's title, consider how it fits with previous chapters, and predict what this reading will cover. In another step, students read the table of contents and decide how this chapter/portion is related to earlier parts. In another step, students read the chapter's introduction and identify the main idea. In another step, students skip to the end of the reading portion or chapter, read the summary, and compose a summary statement. Another step requires students to determine how the chapter is organized by reading its subtitles and other organizational elements, and then write an outline in their own words based on the main headings in the chapter.

Multipass is a learning strategy designed by researchers (Schumaker et al, 1982) to help teenage students with learning disabilities (LD) related to reading. It consists of an initial Survey pass, a medial Size-Up pass, and a final Sort-Out pass. In the second or Size-Up pass, students look for textual cues to aid their comprehension of the text. They review the illustrations (drawings/paintings, maps, graphs, charts, diagrams, etc.) and consider why these are included in the chapter. Then they read the questions provided at the beginning of the chapter, throughout it, and at the end. They mark any questions they can answer at the time. Then students read through the vocabulary words noted in the chapter. After this, they reread the headings within the chapter, which they had reviewed during the initial pass. They ask themselves questions based on the chapter's textual cues, and scan the selection for answers. When they find answers to the questions, they paraphrase them (restate them in their own words).

The Multipass learning strategy (Schumaker et al, 1982) is designed to help students, particularly those in high school who have reading disabilities, to improve their reading comprehension by following steps to access more of the meaning from the text they are reading. They make three passes of a text chapter: One to survey the chapter's title, introduction, table of contents, subtitles, and summary; another to "Size Up" the selection by analyzing textual cues such as illustrations, study questions, vocabulary words; and by reviewing the headings again, generating questions based on them, finding the answers by scanning the chapter, and paraphrasing this information. In the third "Sort-Out" pass, students read each study question provided on the chapter. They then try to answer every question. They mark those they were able to answer. For those they do not know, they scan the outlines they made based on chapter headings in the initial pass to find answers, repeating their scans as needed until they have answered all questions.

Instructing students in any learning or studying strategy

One way of effectively instructing students in any given learning or studying strategy consists of six steps (Sturomski, 1997): (1) First, the teacher should pre-test the students for knowledge of the strategy that s/he wants to teach them, and should engage their motivation and interest for learning this strategy. (2) The teacher should describe the chosen strategy for the students. (3) After describing it, the teacher must model the strategy for the students so they can observe it and then imitate it. (4) The teacher must have the students practice the strategy, and must provide them plenty of time and opportunities for practice until they become familiar and proficient with it. (5) The teacher should give the students feedback as they practice the strategy, to correct and improve their application of it. (6) To enable students to generalize the newly learned strategy across various classes and other settings, the teacher should identify and provide multiple and varied opportunities for the students to apply it in different contexts.

Identifying books according to their levels of age-appropriateness

Some systems used to classify reading materials for the age and grade levels they best apply to are the Basal Level or PALS (Phonological Awareness Literacy Screening) system; the Guided Reading system; the Reading Recovery system; the Developmental Reading Assessment (DRA) level system; and the Rigby PM system. Books for typical kindergarten students are classified at the Readiness level by the PALS/Basal Level system; at Level A in the Guided Reading system; and at Level 1 in Reading Recovery, DRA, and Benchmark 1 in the Rigby PM system. In grades K and/or 1, students are normally at the Continued Readiness level in Basal Level/PALS; level B in Guided Reading; and at Level 2 in the Reading Recovery and DRA systems and Benchmark 2 in the Rigby PM system. Also in grades K/1, reading at the PP1(A) [Preschool-Primary] level in Basal Level/PALS is level C in Guided Reading; 3 and 4 in Reading Recovery; 3 in DRA; and Benchmarks 3 and 4 in Rigby PM.

Classifying books

Various methods classify books by grade, including the Phonological Awareness Literacy Screening (PALS) or Basal Level system; the Guided Reading system; the Reading Recovery system; the Developmental Reading Assessment (DRA) system; and Rigby PM system; and the Lexile Framework, which latter does not apply to early first grade but begins with grade level 1.1. In the PALS system, the preschool/primary level PP2(B) normally applies to first-graders. This level corresponds to level D in the Guided Reading system. In the Reading Recovery system, these correspond with levels 5 and 6. In DRA classification, these are Level 4; and Benchmarks 5 and 6 in the Rigby PM system. Level PP3(C) in PALS corresponds to Level E in Guided Reading; Levels 7 and 8 in Reading Recovery; Levels 6 and 8 in DRA; and Benchmarks 7 and 8 in Rigby PM. In PALS, Level 1.1 for first-graders equals Level F in Guided Reading; 9-10 in Reading Recovery; 10 in DRA; Benchmarks 9 and 10 in Rigby PM; and 200L-400L in the Lexile Framework.

A number of systems have been developed assigning reading levels to books. These include the Phonological Awareness Literacy Screening (PALS)/Basal Level system; the Guided Reading system; the Developmental Reading Assessment (DRA) system; the Rigby PM system; and the Lexile Framework. For second grade, the reading level designated "2.1 continued" by PALS corresponds to Level K in Guided Reading's classification; Level 20 in DRA; Benchmark 18 in Rigby; and Levels 300L-500L in Lexile Framework. The level designated Second/2.2 by PALS corresponds to typical 2nd- and 3rd-grade readers; levels L and M in Guided Reading; Levels 24 and 28 in DRA; Benchmarks 21 and 22 in Rigby PM; and 300L-500L in Lexile Framework. For grades 3-4, PALS uses Third; Guided Reading, Levels N, O, and P; DRA, Levels 30, 34, and 38; Rigby PM, Benchmarks 23, 24, and 25; Lexile Framework, 500L-700L. In fourth grade—Fourth in PALS—Guided Reading uses Levels Q, R, and S; DRA does not apply; Rigby PM assigns Benchmarks 26, 27, and 28, and Lexical Framework 650L-850L.

Categorizing books

Leveling systems that help educators and parents choose texts appropriate for various reading levels include the PALS (Phonological Awareness Literacy Screening)/Basal Level system; the Guided Reading system; the Reading Recovery system; the DRA (Developmental Reading Assessment) system; the Rigby PM system of benchmarks; and the Lexile

Framework. For typical 1st/2nd-grade readers, the PALS level is 1.2, which corresponds to Level H in Guided Reading; Levels 13 and 14 in Reading Recovery; Level 14 in DRA; Benchmark 15 in Rigby PM; and Levels 200L-400 L in the Lexile Framework. 1st- and 2nd-graders at the level deemed 1.2 continued in PALS are at Level I in Guided Reading; Levels 15, 16, and 17 in Reading Recovery; Level 16 in DRA; Benchmark 16 in Rigby PM; and Levels 200L-400L in the Lexile Framework. Second-graders at Level 2.1 in PALS are at Level J in Guided Reading; Levels 18, 19, and 20 in Reading Recovery; Level 18 in DRA; Benchmark 17 in Rigby PM; and Levels 300L-500L in the Lexile Framework.

Discuss the Common Core State Standards (CCSS)

The Common Core State Standards are the result of the CCSS Initiative. They are a set of rigorous, internationally benchmarked standards for American students. Heretofore, each U.S. state had an individual set of standards for public school education, creating varying state expectations at the same grade levels for student achievement. This lack of uniformity created confusion regarding what students needed for college and employment. The CCSS Initiative was coordinated by the National Governors Association Center for Best Practices and the Council of Chief State School Officers. The standards produced were developed through collaborating with teachers, school administrators and educational experts. As of April 2012, the CCSS were adopted by 45 of 50 U.S. states. The CCSS are intended to define the English language arts and mathematics skills and knowledge required to be taught and learned in grades K-12 for students to be equipped for college preparation and work training programs. They include requirements for literacy in social studies/history, science, and technical subjects as well as language arts and reading.

Until recently, each U.S. state has had its own set of academic standards: there was no uniform standard for what K-12 teachers were expected to teach and students to learn to prepare students for college and/or employment. To address this situation, two national organizations representing state educational interests developed the CCSS Initiative to provide uniform K-12 standards for all states, which the majority of states have adopted. These standards give requirements for both ELA and content-area literacy. Content-area literacy standards are not meant to replace content standards but complement them. K-5 standards apply across the disciplines. 6-12 ELA and content-area standards promote the concept of sharing responsibility across disciplines for developing literacy. Requiring literacy across the curriculum is a change from existing state reading and ELA standards. Consequently, teachers must: expect all students to participate actively; promote learning processes instead of simply giving information; demonstrate their expertise in content-area literacy; carefully structure situations for independent student problem-solving; and encourage students to discover solutions, not depend on adults to provide them.

One characteristic of education as determined by the CCSS is that in grades K-5, students' reading should balance literary and informational texts, such that at least half of their reading is informational. In elementary schools, children encounter social studies, the sciences, the arts, and literature through reading texts. Through reading in these content areas, young students gain access to the world. According to this criterion, student activities include building their content knowledge; gaining exposure to the world via reading; and applying various strategies. Teacher activities include balancing informational and literary text; supplying scaffolding (support) with informational texts; and teaching both *with* and *through* informational texts. Grade 6-12 content-area teachers must stress literacy experiences in their curriculum and instruction; conceive of their work as teaching reading, not just their subjects; substitute reading for references and summaries; and slow down science and history classes. Students are expected to learn from their reading, not simply refer to texts; to build content knowledge further; work with primary sources; and locate evidence.

The CCSS were developed to create uniform educational standards across U.S. states to prepare students for higher education and employment. One aspect of this preparation is that texts used in colleges and jobs are more complex than K-12 texts. The standards thus require teachers to assign texts that gradually increase in complexity with each grade level. Teachers must, therefore, also exercise more patience, and allow and arrange more time and space in their curricula for closer, more careful, and more in-depth reading. They will need to assign smaller amounts of reading to do this. They should provide students with strategies to facilitate deeper reading of more complex text, and with scaffolding—i.e., needed support that they gradually decrease as students gain proficiency. Teachers should also engage with other adults over texts. Students are called upon to re-read texts; to read on their own levels, for enjoyment; and to develop more tolerance for the frustration they will experience with reading more difficult text.

The CCSS place more emphasis than previous, individual state educational standards on students' developing the ability to defend their arguments with text-based answers. To meet this standard, students must learn to locate proof/evidence in the text to support their assertions. They must develop into scholars and formulate their own judgments. They need to read text more closely. And they must also engage with the authors of the texts they read, and the choices made by authors. To help students meet these criteria, teachers must keep students focused on the text, and insist that all associated classroom experiences remain deeply connected to the text. Teachers should plan and lead rich conversations about the text, and promote discussions based on evidence in the text. Teachers should identify questions that will stimulate discussion among the students, that are also worthwhile, and that depend on the text to be discussed and answered. Teachers will also need to devote more time to their class preparation by reading the text more deeply themselves.

The developers of the CCSS advise that while narrative is important, students must also develop skills for writing argument and persuasion that they support through text-based information. This information includes not only facts and events, but also ideas and arguments that students encounter in the texts they read. To write from textual sources, students must be able to generate their own informational text. They must learn to use evidence from texts to back up their arguments, to organize their writing to persuade the reader, and to compare multiple sources. To teach them these skills, teachers must spend less time on having students write personal narratives, and give students opportunities for writing using multiple research sources. They should give students opportunities to analyze/break down and synthesize/put together ideas they encounter. They must help students develop their own voices for arguing points using evidence. They should offer students permission to arrive at their own conclusions about what they read and articulate these conclusions.

Reading increasingly complex texts

Since common core standards have been created for all U.S. states and adopted by most of them, the emphasis in teaching academic vocabulary is shifting, from teaching literary terms (e.g., *alliteration* or *onomatopoeia*) that are less practical for content-area literacy and literacy across the curriculum, to teaching more commonly occurring and essential words (e.g., *theory, principled, generation,* and *discourse*). As textbooks become more and more complex with ascending grade levels, students must have general skills to be able to read and comprehend them across the various content area disciplines. To do this, students will need to build their databases of vocabulary reflecting words that are powerful across academic and workplace disciplines. They will also need to use such "language of power" words across content areas in speech and writing. To facilitate these student tasks, teachers must develop student abilities for accessing and using words; strategically focus on the most critical, prevalent new vocabulary words; concentrate on words students will use most; and teach students fewer words, but more in-depth.

Information books

Information books are books whose main intent is to report facts about the nature of a certain thing, such as weather or rocks; or of a particular genus or species of plant or animal. Four required elements of the information genre are: (1) topic presentation; (2) descriptive attributes; (3) characteristic events, describing typical processes, events, or actions that the topic is engaged in or does; and (4) final summary. Eight additional elements, which are optional rather than required, are (1) a prelude; (2) comparison(s) of different categories, types, or instances of the topic; (3) historical vignette(s); (4) experimental idea(s); (5) an afterword; (6) addenda; (7) a recapitulation; and (8) illustration extension(s). In addition, the information genre has certain features. These include a table of contents; headings; diagrams; pictures and photographs; captions; the use of a technical vocabulary; the use of generic nouns; the use of the timeless present tense; a glossary of terms; and an index.

Elementary school teachers are realizing that informational texts are important for developing children's reading and writing skills. Research finds that elementary students' knowledge of both content and genre is supported by experience with informational books, and that they use elements of this genre in their own writing from early ages. Research also implies that teachers' reading information books aloud and explicitly teaching genre elements to young students improves their instruction. Moreover, instructing students to "think like writers" as they read builds their knowledge about authors' organizational decision-making processes. Some teachers realized their students had read information texts, discussed them, written short book reports, and constructed projects about them, but never written their own information books. They assigned this, preparing students with focused read-aloud sessions explicitly analyzing the genre elements and features in the text, and systematically teaching them how to apply these in their own writing. They found this effective in helping students learn to read and write in diverse forms and for multiple audience—skills needed to communicate effectively.

Promoting student motivation to read

Researchers find that what teachers do in class can significantly affect student motivation to read. Some identified practices and their results include (cf. McRae and Guthrie, 2009): Teachers' assigning and allowing reading relevant to students promote interest and internal motivation. Teachers' allowing and inviting student choices of reading promote student ownership. Teachers' enabling student success promotes student self-efficacy (a sense of competence to succeed at tasks). Teachers' provision of collaboration promotes students' social interactions with their peers. Teachers' provision of thematic units promotes student mastery of content. Practices that undermine motivation include: Teachers' assigning material irrelevant to students promotes avoidance of reading. Teachers' exercising excessive control promotes low student ownership of reading. Teachers' assigning overly difficult lessons promotes student perceptions of excessive difficulty. Teachers' frequently assigning individual work promotes student isolation, undermining social interaction. Teachers' introducing disconnected units rather than thematically organized ones undermines student interest in meaning and mastery, and promotes student avoidance of working for mastery of reading and of its content.

Combined text books

Traditionally, two major genres of books have been narrative, i.e. stories, and expository, i.e. informational. The combined-text genre, however, uses a combination of narrative and expository formats within one book. In the *Magic School Bus* series, for instance, fantasy stories like a class field trip to the ocean floor (Cole, 1992) are combined with information like reference charts and reports included in illustrations of the classroom. In *Snowflake Bentley* (Martin, 1998), the biography of Bentley is narrative; the specialized photography technique he developed is explained through informational margin notes. *Stellaluna* (Cannon, 1993) tells a fantasy narrative, followed by informational text about the characters' real-life equivalents. *Cook-a-Doodle-Doo!* (Stevens & Crummel, 1999) integrates exposition about using cookbooks and cooking with narrative about farm animals making strawberry shortcake. Both students and teachers can become distracted by multiple concepts and overwhelmed about navigating contrasting formats; elementary students cannot differentiate fantasy from scientific concepts. The solution, which also makes reading most effective, is to read these books in layers: illustrations; information; narrative; and additional details.

Combined-text books, incorporating narrative and informational formats within the same book, can expand student knowledge bases about diverse topics, also giving students experience applying this knowledge to fictional/fantasy stories. Teachers should closely observe concepts shared between both formats. Then, using various strategies during reading, rereading, and reviewing a book, teachers can improve student abilities to develop concepts, facts, and stories simultaneously. Experts recommend (1) reading the Illustrations layer, using a picture walk before reading to activate and/or develop schemata and stimulate student questions and comments on the informational topic; and the Pre-Reading Plan (PReP) to elicit and address student questions or misconceptions. (2) Reading the informational layer can be facilitated using the "zoom in, zoom out" strategy to identify salient concepts; and concept of definition (CD) maps to help students recognize concept interrelationships and levels. (3) Reading the narrative layer is aided by interactive read-alouds and creating story maps. (4) Reading the additional details layer, e.g., sketches and page borders, is supported by semantic maps and shared writing exercises.

Developing interdisciplinary units or writing across the curriculum has historically required combining narrative, informational, and pictorial texts into text sets on a specific topic. An advantage of combined-text books is that teachers can use them as focal texts to connect other books to the topic. For example, teachers can use other books in the text set throughout their unit, and a combined-text book for read-alouds. Using strategies appropriate to each layer of a combined-text book will inform students of the purposes of reading specific texts, and show them how strategic reading builds on their existing areas of concept knowledge. Teaching layers with associated strategies also helps students and teachers more easily identify target, superordinate, coordinate, and subordinate concepts. Clear identification of these helps teachers utilize materials optimally to meet state and national educational standards. Individual read-alouds for each layer allow teachers to model revisiting text for different purposes. Students more easily develop teacher-targeted concepts through reading individual layers, and establish fundamental knowledge for recognizing and differentiating fact from fantasy.

Benefits of teaching expository book structures

The majority of preschool and primary school teachers are familiar with the story elements found in storybooks and other narrative texts. Many young children are also familiar with stories when they begin school, and most younger students quickly learn to identify and remember such story structures. Similarly to narrative texts, informational texts also use certain structures that teachers can teach young students to recognize. Teachers can use such expository structures to improve younger students' comprehension, which researchers have found will further benefit their understanding of content-area texts written at intermediate and higher levels. Studies have concluded that the role of the teacher is crucial in order for students to interact effectively with informational texts in the classroom. Teachers must both possess strong knowledge about informational texts, and provide their students with greater access to such books. Teachers can consult online references prepared by experts to help them make selections that have high quality and appeal highly to younger readers' interests.

Children's books

Publication of children's literature has exploded in the early 21st century. While this provides a huge array of books available, it also requires teachers to make more informed choices from the flood of material. Fortunately, scholars and education experts have provided a number of guides and checklists, available online, to help them choose. Researchers have found that young children must encounter a diversity of text types to succeed in developing literacy. They have also concluded that children's language skills grow more widely when their teachers regularly include informational texts in their classrooms in an authentic way. As young children naturally are curious, elementary-school teachers spend much time answering their questions; and reading books aloud to them daily, enriching their vocabularies and relating the reading to children's prior knowledge. Informational texts can enhance both activities, as well as give teachers valued resources. Also, numerous experts find that smoother transitions between elementary and intermediate reading levels are afforded by incorporating broadly varied books, including emphasizing informational texts equally.

The cover of a book, being the first thing children see, should capture their attention and invite them to look inside. Experts find that illustrations or photographs that are clear and colorful, and that use bright, primary colors, are most attractive to younger children. In addition to the colors and illustrations, the book's title should grab a child's attention and should stimulate interest and inquiry in young readers. Titles should be brief enough to engage them, using words they can understand and fonts large enough for them to read easily. For example, some quality informational books which feature covers that catch children's eyes and grab their attention include *Big Bugs* (Simon, 2005); *Fishy Tales* (Lock, 2003); and *Bats* (Wood, 2000). Publishers of children's books such as Dorling Kindersley and National Geographic have recently issued books with covers and titles that entice children's attention and interest, setting an excellent example for the many other publishers of children's literature.

Non-fiction books need not be dull. Young children tend to be naturally interested in many topics covered in children's literature, and their inquisitive nature attracts them to information to answer their myriad questions about life and the world. However, there are still aspects of these books that will make them even more interesting to children. Parents and teachers should look for topics in books that their children find exciting, and which include a bit of mystery as well. Authors who share fascinating factual information in the manner of tour guides will invite children to follow them into the "jungle" of information. Because our current times are considered the "information age," it is important to give children reliable and accurate content. Adults should look for authors' documentation of references, sources, and/or consultations with experts in the areas covered by their books. One example of an author highly regarded by educational experts is Seymour Simon, who has written over 200 high-quality books about diverse topics like storms, earthquakes, sharks, trucks, etc.

Just as museum displays, educational TV shows and movies must balance factual information that interests viewers with visual effects that fascinate them, so too must informational children's books balance interesting facts with fascinating visual illustrations. In high-quality children's nonfiction, all of the illustrations should be large and clear, and not excessively "busy" or crowded. Including photographs is always an important part of nonfiction. Light-colored or white backgrounds help add contrast to photos to be more appealing to children. The illustrations should explain the book's content and enhance it. Also, any included captions and/or labels should be simple, and yet should also name or explain the illustrations sufficiently. A good example of watercolor illustrations that support the text is in Pallotta's (1987) *The Bird Alphabet Book*. Two examples of children's books that incorporate colorful photographs that reinforce their text content include Meharry's (2001) *Mud, Mud, Mud* and Cowley's (2005) *Chameleon, Chameleon*.

How children's books are organized can provide the same benefits to young readers as directing signs in buildings or road maps. Good organization guides readers through books, helping them alternate attention effortlessly between text and illustrations and browse interesting topics. An informational book should, when applicable, include a table of contents, glossary of terms/vocabulary words, and index. Divisions between sections should be clear; headings and subheadings should be included as needed. For younger children who read independently, a good example of a well-organized book is Reid & Chessen's (1998) *Bugs, Bugs, Bugs!* It clearly separates illustrations from text; identifies one insect body part per page; and closes with two pages of interesting facts about insects and a basic index. Another example, for older children to read independently and younger children to browse and learn facts or read with adults, is Adams' (2001) *The Best Book of Volcanoes.* It opens with a pictorial table of contents; clearly divides topics, subtopics, text, and illustrations; and includes an illustrated glossary and an index.

When selecting information books for young readers, adults should appraise not only their covers, topics, content, illustrations, and organization, but also attributes like font size, type, placement, and spacing. For younger children, letters should be larger than for adults or older children, with a clear and simple type style. Smaller letters are hard for young children to read, and unusual lettering styles are distracting for beginning readers. Also, words, and spaces between letters and words, should be placed on the page to ensure optimal reading ease. For inexperienced readers, anything less straightforward will impede reading comprehension. Young readers should be able to follow text on each page without effort. Publishers have recently produced many informational book series with brief, simple content, which young readers can easily read on their own. The *Scholastic Time to Discover* series has these characteristics. For example, one of its titles, Berger and Berger's (2002) *Ants, Bees, and Butterflies* includes a large font, consistent letter placement and spacing, and an easy reading level.

Teen/young adult literature

One way teachers integrate teen/young adult literature into the curriculum is using core texts, of various genres but particularly novels that the whole class reads and studies together. This is likely the most popular current method for studying literature in middle and high school. This approach gives teachers more control, but may limit student participation in discussions about literature. However, effective teachers still manage to engage students in whole-class discussions about a selected book and associated major concepts ("big ideas"). Another method teachers use to organize literature study is compiling text sets from which students select. This approach features fewer whole-class discussions and more book-club/literature-circle conversations. The multiple-text approach appears to afford more student engagement, active participation, and deeper appreciation of literature, likely through giving students more classroom "voice and choice." A third method used by most middle- and high-school teachers is incorporating independent student reading, via silent classroom reading periods and/or assigning home reading. Experts also recommend reading workshops as an effective way to integrate independent reading.

One way that teachers incorporate young adult literature into their curricula is to follow the organization often used in literature anthology textbooks and isolate different literary genres, studying one genre of text at a time. According to some experts, the drawback of this approach is that the curriculum ends up lacking in cohesion, which makes it harder for students to compare, contrast, relate, and connect various literary works. Another approach used by some middle- and high-school teachers includes two methods: (1) They design thematic units incorporating multiple literary genres. They select books that share a common theme, across various genres. This enables students to explore major concepts ("big ideas") and establish connections among different genres of literature. (2) These teachers create interdisciplinary units, wherein they are able to collaborate with teachers of other content areas. This offers the advantages of erasing or softening some of the school system curriculum's artificial divisions, and of enabling teachers to work with each other and their students in exploring ideas.

Patricia Polacco, an author with a multicultural background, wrote and illustrated *Mr. Lincoln's Way* (2001) about an African-American school principal and a bullying student from a white supremacist family. The child loves the principal but is afraid to interact with him because of his and his family's perspective. The author comments that when skin color is an issue, people must find something they share in common. The boy and principal find this common ground in a shared love of birds. The principal uses the love of birds of all colors as an analogy to teach the student to eschew racist comments about others. The author remarks about her book's messages about diversity, acceptance, and tolerance that "it doesn't matter how different we are. There is something we can find that we have in common. And that should be the place that we start from, our commonality. And then from there, we celebrate our difference instead of having difference be a cause for a feeling of isolation."

Multicultural literature

Literature in general, and particularly multicultural literature, gives young people exposure to customs, traditions, beliefs, and values that they will not be exposed to at home. It can also give them an understanding of these diverse cultural aspects they would not otherwise have. When children and adolescents read authentic stories from other cultures, they realize that people are essentially the same at heart, regardless of outward appearances and behaviors. This is a great benefit in helping to shape children into world citizens in times of increasing globalization. While some children grow up in multicultural neighborhoods, those who do not lack the experience of understanding why other people look, dress, talk, eat, pray, and do other things differently. Literature can supply this experience. Many cultures have oral traditions of storytelling; children having this custom in their families learn how things were in the past; and they gain senses of their place, their birth order, and of being loved even before birth.

Computer technology

While educators may think classroom computers are new educational innovations, these have actually been present for over 20 years. The first recorded instance of 1:1 laptops was in 1990. In the late 1990s, Microsoft's Anytime Anywhere Learning Program initiative introduced laptops to a thousand schools. Over half of American schools had some laptops by 2005. Since their introduction, researchers have found laptops and Internet connections supply scaffolding to students for many classroom topics, building students' background knowledge. Researchers also observed greater student engagement in wireless classes, which included analysis of reading, more varied writing activities, and using software to produce media. Moreover, research has found that students attained control over reading, both on computer screens and book pages. Students in wireless classrooms discover technology has more to offer them than texting and gaming, like knowing how navigate, search for and locate information, and interpreting visual and textual elements in documents. Because today's kids see technology simply as life, education connected to their lives by technology is more engaging and motivating.

Much instructional software exists today. For example, KidBiz Achieve 3000 is a web-based individualized reading and writing instructional program. Students each receive KidBiz e-mails with questions designed to activate their background knowledge prior to reading current events articles. Multiple articles on the same topics are provided at different reading levels: all students in a class read similar articles, but each at his/her own reading level. After replying to answer the e-mailed question, students read the article. This software also helps teachers prepare students for high-stakes, standardized, criterion-referenced tests (CRTs). The KidBiz website provides "thought questions" that supply writing prompts related to its provided articles and require students to write constructed-response questions based on what they read, similar to CRT questions. Teachers assign small-group/whole-class discussions following these activities. Students find lists of all stories their class is reading that year on a webpage, which links to a website such as Flashcard Exchange, where teachers have entered vocabulary words for each story. Students can study/practice the words for any story they select.

In a class using technology, a teacher gives an elementary school class (4th-graders, for example) an open-ended question—e.g., about an imaginary friend—and have students IM their assigned "buddy" describing him/her/it. The teacher leads class discussion about the writing trait Ideas and Content; then has them listen for examples of this as s/he reads them a picture book about an imaginary friend. The teacher has students visit a website such as www.writingfix.com, which offers interactive writing prompts guiding students to describe the imaginary friend's specific characteristics. This prepares students for a "Quick Write" (first draft). As they write, the teacher discusses individual writing and improvements with some students. Students' Quick Writes are electronically saved for revisiting and advancing through further drafts. Students use built-in software features like spell-check, grammar-check, and thesaurus for editing, learning mindfulness when they find software is not always right. Peer review is also facilitated electronically. Students print and post finished writing on the bulletin board. Such activities show smooth transitions from traditional to new literacies.

RAFT

RAFT is a strategy that helps students to understand what topic they will be writing about, what audience(s) they will be addressing in their writing, the different writing formats, and their own roles as writers. Some advantages of RAFT are that it helps students learn essential writing skills like main idea, organization, and audience; incorporates writing from various perspectives; can be applied across different content areas; and teaches students creative thinking about writing. Students learn to think creatively about writing as they respond to these prompts, which form the acronym: **R**ole of the writer—As the writer, who are you—a soldier, pilgrim, president? etc.; **A**udience—Whom are you addressing in your writing—your teacher, your friend, newspaper readers? etc.; **F**ormat—What format are you writing in—a poem, a letter, a speech? etc.; and **T**opic (and strong verb)—About what are you writing? Why? What is the point and/or topic? RAFT can be used before, during, and after reading; and with individual students, small groups, or whole classes.

RAFT stands for Role of the writer, Audience for the writing, Format of the writing, and Topic of the writing. It is a strategy that teachers can use to help students learn their role, i.e. who they as the writers are; who their audiences of readers will be; the different types of formats available in which they can write; and what topics they will be addressing in their writing. It helps students to practice writing for different purposes and various audiences, to think about topics from different perspectives, and to write creatively. To use RAFT, a teacher first shows the class a finished writing example using RAFT on an overhead projector. The teacher describes each element (Role, Audience, Format, and Topic) using simple examples, which s/he may write on the board/overhead/easel. The teacher models writing responses for the prompt associated with each element and discusses these with the class. The teacher then has students practice writing their own prompt responses, individually or in small groups.

Purposes, characteristics and benefits of writing

While we use writing as a tool to communicate, learn, document, gather, and circulate information; and to express our thoughts and feelings and persuade others, writing is actually more than a way of expressing ourselves and communicating. Research findings indicate that, as with reading, instruction is necessary for learning how to write well; and that, also as with reading, improving our writing skills improves our ability to learn.

Additionally, the relationship of writing and reading is reciprocal: skills like spelling and grammar needed for writing are reinforced by having good reading skills; and having good writing skills in turn reinforces reading skills. Education experts identify these characteristics of good writers: They can read and write across different disciplines and genres. They use varied strategies in the writing process. They learn to be goal-oriented and self-directed in writing. They apply self-regulation strategies to help themselves independently plan, organize, and revise their writing, e.g., setting goals, self-monitoring, and self-instruction. They recognize and can compose in genres like descriptive, persuasive, and narrative writing.

Improving student writing skills

Research shows that the practice found most effective to improve student writing skills is systematic, direct, and explicit instruction in writing. Studies find that when high school teachers teach students the skills and strategies that promote writing development, they are able to build on students' existing knowledge, and to introduce new information in context. Teachers can instruct high school students to plan, draft, revise, and edit their compositions as steps in the writing process, and teach them the skills needed for revision and editing, across the content areas of the curriculum. Systematic, direct, explicit writing instruction includes these steps: (1) Teachers explain each skill or strategy, and model its application in writing in a way similar to what they will assign students to do. (2) Teachers give students guidance in using these skills and strategies in writing assignments, and supply corrective feedback. (3) Teachers give students opportunities and time to practice the skills and strategies independently. (4) Teachers repeat these steps until students can use them all independently when writing.

Writing process

The steps of the writing process are planning, drafting, revising, and editing. Two common problems with students are that they do not do any planning before starting to write; and that they do not edit or revise after writing something. Research finds that planning, or pre-writing, gives students time to determine what they know about the writing topic and to organize their thoughts; this is true in any content area. Planning also enables students to determine what they may need to research about a topic, and to figure out how they are going to organize their report or essay. Three planning strategies that are frequently used are (1) brainstorming and making lists; (2) making outlines; and (3) using graphic organizers. These pre-writing activities can enable students to take their loosely organized ideas and thoughts and form them into structures that they can use to verbalize them more effectively.

Helping high school students prepare to write

One reason some adolescents struggle with writing is that they fail to plan before writing. Consequently they can produce writing that is disorganized, omits necessary information, and fails to make important connections. To remedy this, teachers can guide them in using pre-writing or planning strategies. Brainstorming elicits more of what students already know about a topic, and helps them generate more ideas about it. Teachers should encourage students to think and speak freely. Brainstorming is not a time for editing. Later on, teachers will guide students to select only the most topic-relevant items from their brainstorming lists. Making lists helps students keep track of all ideas, some of which they would otherwise forget. Making outlines helps students structure their ideas. For teens struggling with reading, outlines should not be elaborate or overly detailed. They could have only three tiers, for example: main topics, subtopics, and supporting details. Graphic organizers like compare-contrast matrices, spider maps, cause-effect, and series-of-events chains help students visualize relationships and connections in their information.

Having students publish their writing

Among educators involved in literacy instruction, many view students' publishing their writing as a way to achieve closure and satisfaction at the end of a successful teaching unit focused on writing fictional work. Teachers find that most students derive considerable pride from producing and seeing a finished piece of their own creative writing efforts. In addition to providing visible, tangible copies of their individual ideas and hard work, publication can also afford students a means of sharing with their families the special quality of the creative writing process and its results. Another good rationale for allowing and assigning students to publish their writing is its value in motivating students to revise and proofread their own work. Without knowing that it will be distributed for others to see, they would be less likely to make the additional efforts of preparing their own writing to make it fit for publication.

Science publication

When professional scientists have completed an investigation or an experiment, in writing up their findings and conclusions in preparation for publishing, they frequently must create summaries of the work they have completed for readers who have little knowledge about the particular field of study. Therefore, researchers and scientists must be able to express their own knowledge in ways understandable to all readers. In the same way, science students must be able to relate the things they have found and learned so that everybody can understand it. Two actions required of any scientist, including students, in reporting and publication, are: summarizing the information they have acquired; and explaining that information clearly and simply. To summarize, teachers can help students begin with the "big picture." For example, have them state the purpose of their experiment; e.g., "to measure local rainfall in the past month." Then have them provide facts supporting this purpose, e.g., they made a rain gauge; materials used; daily monitoring, measurement recording, gauge emptying, measurement graphing, etc.

After scientists ask a research question, design an experiment or investigation using chosen methods, and conduct their research, they must write reports of what they found and their conclusions based on these findings for publication in order to disseminate the knowledge they have gained. Publishing scientific results includes: (1) summarizing one's work clear to be understood by readers not necessarily knowledgeable about the area of study; and (2) explaining the procedures and methods they followed using clear and descriptive language. Young science students must do the same things, which helps develop their cognitive processes, in both the scientific method and literacy. In addition to guiding students in summarizing the main idea and itemizing the facts of their procedures, teachers can guide students to use descriptive definitions and words to characterize their experiment/investigations. They can review vocabulary words they discussed during their research. For example, if students built a gauge to measure rainfall, they can define the word "gauge" and discuss terms like drought, drizzling, pouring rain, etc.

When young scientists have gathered all of the data from the research or experiment they have conducted, adults can help them share what they have learned by suggesting combined methods, such as writing; dictating; and making drawings, diagrams, graphs, etc., to summarize, simplify, and share the information they have acquired. Adults can remind children to state their topic of study; to present facts that support what they found out; and to state their conclusions. To make scientific learning exercises more enjoyable and creative, adults can suggest that children write a mock newspaper article including a catchy headline, a short descriptive paragraph, and the graph they produced during their research. Teachers and parents can also help young scientists to use various digital tools, like blogging services and photo sharing services, in producing and publishing what they write about their research; these make writing and publication easier and more motivating. Another benefit of publication is allowing children to reflect on their work and share it with others, completing the scientific process.

Tier 1, 2 and 3 vocabulary words

Tier 1 words are those used in everyday conversation, like *house* or *car*. Tier 2 words are often used in mature language, less in everyday speech but more in writing. These can strongly affect verbal functioning and well adapted to teaching during read-aloud interactions. Tier 3 words are academic vocabulary, usually taught during content-area lessons. In vocabulary instruction, teacher focus levels include: (1) incidentally exposing students to new words; (2) embedding instruction in discussion; and (3) focusing instruction on vocabulary. To expose students incidentally to words, the teacher incorporates Tier 2 words into discussions of read-alouds; e.g., "He wanted to know; his *curiosity* got the better of him." In embedding instruction, the teacher gives a synonym to define a word, and points at the book's illustration of it, e.g., "He's using a stick, called an *oar*, [pointing] to move the boat." In focused instruction, the teacher might define "get set" as getting ready, leading a discussion with students giving examples of things they get set for, like holidays or school.

Incidental exposure, embedded instruction, and focused instruction

Before, during, and after a teacher reads a story aloud to the class, s/he uses incidental exposure by incorporating less familiar words in discussions and providing contextual clues to their meanings. For instance, the teacher might describe characters as "coming bearing gifts;" or as "humble." This instructional level builds vocabulary knowledge without direct instruction. When target vocabulary words are not central to the story, and/or they express concepts the students recognize, teachers use embedded instruction, giving information about the words' meanings via short definitions or synonyms, interrupting the reading-aloud flow as little as possible. When vocabulary words are essential to comprehending the story, and/or when students have trouble comprehending their meaning, teachers use focused instruction. This includes a wide range of teacher-student interactions, from 4-25 instances, and frequently occurs before or after reading. It may depend on keywords that teachers have identified; and/or it may consist of spontaneous teacher responses to students' confusion and/or questions during the reading.

Definitional, contextual, and conceptual types of vocabulary knowledge

A teacher's learning goal for his/her young students influences the characteristics of instructional activities using read-alouds and discussions. When the goal is just to expose students to a new word, and/or when students are familiar with a word's conceptual basis, teachers use the definitional approach—giving students a definitional phrase or a synonym for a word, or eliciting these from students. This is a time-efficient approach, permitting teachers to address many words during read-alouds. When teachers have students refer to the text to ascertain a word's meaning, they are developing students' contextual word knowledge. They may reread a word's sentence context to help students prove or disprove their ideas of its meaning. For students to develop in-depth word comprehension, learning definitions is usually insufficient; they need conceptual knowledge to connect new words with words they already know and with their previous experiences. Teachers develop concepts via examples and questioning before reading; reinforcing definitions during reading; and giving students opportunities to use new words in various other contexts.

Teaching young students new vocabulary words

Common instructional strategies teachers use to help young students learn new vocabulary words include: (1) Questioning – when reading aloud, teachers stop at unfamiliar words, asking students their meanings. They may also (2) supply definitions and typical applications, asking students for corresponding words, most often in embedded instruction. To elicit targeted words and reinforce word learning, teachers often (3) provide synonyms. Another strategy to clarify and expand word knowledge is (4) giving students and/or eliciting from them examples of target words. This offers opportunities to use target words; and helps students learn relationships to other words and concepts, and connect words to instances of their use. Teachers also (5) correct and/or clarify student responses, completing partial understandings and/or addressing misunderstandings to guide vocabulary knowledge; (6) extend students' word definitions, supplementing their information; (7) labeling picture-book illustrations with corresponding new words; (8) using facial, gestural, and/or auditory imagery to illustrate word meanings during read-alouds; and (9) teaching morphemic analyses of complex new words for roots and other components to figure out meanings.

To optimize students' ability to learn new word meanings, experts recommend that teachers use the following steps, identified through research into effective teacher practices: (1) Before reading, identify words in the text that (a) are central to comprehension, (b) are Tier 2 words to build students' reading vocabulary, and (c) are interesting and/or fun to say; and target 4-5 words for teaching more in-depth comprehension. (2) Ascertain the kind of vocabulary learning needed: incidental, embedded, or focused instruction; before, during, or after reading; and strategies to apply, by identifying familiar words used in new ways; new words for familiar concepts; words expressing new/unfamiliar concepts; and words essential to comprehension. (3) Identify instructional strategies commensurate with learning goals—e.g., synonyms/gestures with new words for familiar terms; pre-reading questioning and examples to develop new concepts; simple definitions during reading to reinforce learning. (4) Prepare a "Plan B" if a strategy fails, e.g., giving clarifications, corrections, synonyms, examples, and simple definitions. (5) Incorporate new vocabulary words learned into other classroom contexts.

Importance of vocabulary development to student reading skills

For close to a century, researchers have recognized students' vocabulary learning as significantly predictive of their reading comprehension. More recently, research also finds general reading performance and school achievement highly predicted by vocabulary knowledge. Researchers have also noted that students' decoding skills are predicted by their receptive vocabulary development. Students who know more words can read and comprehend text more easily. However, students typically enter school with widely varying levels of vocabulary knowledge. This variation is increased by students' diverse socioeconomic backgrounds and/or cognitive capacities. Research finds such variance across school grades; therefore, without intervention, differences among students only increase, so lower-performing students find catching up with age/grade peers more difficult. Moreover, students with reading problems demonstrate greater comprehension gains through vocabulary instruction than students without reading problems. Thus, educational experts advise integrating vocabulary into daily literacy instruction as crucial. To improve reading comprehension, teaching vocabulary should include both word definitions and contexts; engage students in deep processing; and offer students multiple exposures to the same words.

Integrating progressively more sophisticated vocabulary words

Researchers have described an effective fourth-grade teacher's use of a daily, morning greeting activity, which was not only important to her classroom management plan and to building the classroom community, but moreover provided engaging vocabulary-learning experiences. Each student would greet the classmate to his/her left using a positive descriptor. Students began with simple adjectives like "nice," "talented," and "happy." Over time, the teacher encouraged them to use more original synonyms, like "friendly," "creative," and "jolly." Eventually, the teacher modeled the greeting using more sophisticated synonyms, like "affable," "virtuous," and "jovial." These unfamiliar words motivated students to look them up in dictionaries to understand their meanings, which they then remembered through associating them with real classmates. This strategy also motivated students to make greater efforts to use more sophisticated adjectives each time they performed the greeting activity. Students soon were comfortable using large descriptive lexicons; soon thereafter, the teacher observed them using these words in classroom discussions, casual conversations, and writing assignments, proving their word ownership, application, and generalization.

Types of vocabulary

Educational researchers have defined vocabulary as oral, print, receptive, and productive. When children listen to speech—including being read aloud to—and produce speech, they understand and use oral vocabulary words. When they read and/or write, they use print vocabulary. When they are listening or reading, they are using receptive vocabulary. When they are speaking or writing, they are using productive vocabulary. Researchers find that students' productive vocabulary words are more familiar, better known, and used more often than are words in their receptive vocabularies. They also observe that children's receptive vocabularies are bigger than their productive vocabularies, and that receptive vocabulary is essential to children's early reading development. As children learn to decode printed words in texts, they apply their existing vocabulary knowledge to attain comprehension of what they are reading. Therefore, if words in the text they read are not included in their vocabularies, young readers will not understand the text. Thus it is crucial to develop children's early vocabularies for them to read with comprehension.

Children's vocabulary development

Experts find children's word knowledge is not black-and-white, i.e. simply knowing/not knowing a word's meaning, but a continuum of how much a student knows about a word, from a little to a lot. One classification of vocabulary knowledge (Dale, 1965) has four levels: (1) never heard/saw the word before; (2) heard/saw the word but does not know its meaning; (3) recognizes the word within context as related to some concept/topic/meaning; and (4) knows the word well. Another classification (Beck et al, 1987) identifies five levels along the continuum: (1) no knowledge of the word; (2) general idea; (3) narrow, contextually-dependent knowledge; (4) some knowledge, but unable to retrieve the word for suitable applications; and (5) rich, context-independent knowledge of word meaning. While some researchers advocate deeper understanding of fewer words, to apply vocabulary learned during writing and speaking as well as reading; and others emphasize acquiring greater vocabulary breadth for comprehending diverse texts, the majority agree that *both* depth and breadth are important to children's word knowledge.

Vocabulary development in elementary and secondary school students

Researchers have found that typically, a third-grade student knows approximately 8,000 vocabulary words, while a typical high-school student knows 25,000-50,000 or more words. Most students learn 3,000-4,000 new words every year. Vocabulary instruction therefore is a giant undertaking, given the numbers of new words a student acquires annually. Four essential elements of vocabulary instruction (Graves, 2000) are (1) reading widely; (2) teaching individual words; (3) strategies for learning words; and (4) developing word consciousness. Word consciousness is defined as being aware of words and their meanings; being interested in these; being aware of how and when new vocabulary words are used; being motivated to learn new words, and being able to use newly learned words with skill. Across all grade and age levels, it is critical for teachers to support development of students' word consciousness, particularly in those students who have previously had limited exposure to sufficient volume, variety, breadth, and depth of vocabulary.

Promoting word consciousness

Students from backgrounds of economic poverty, in both rural and urban areas, and those who are English-language learners (ELLs), have fewer chances to learn English vocabulary words at home. However, effective teachers have developed word consciousness— including strong motivation to learn more new words—in these students. These teachers used such practices as providing word-rich environments and enabling students' success and enjoyment in learning new words throughout the curriculum and school year. Consequently, these students noticed unfamiliar words used by others and asked their meanings; and they identified new words they had learned when they heard them being used in various contexts, connecting them with other words and gaining deeper comprehension of the new words. Researchers find that such word consciousness strongly eases the challenge of students' learning thousands of new words annually—particularly because research also finds that a major agent of children's vocabulary growth is incidental, contextual learning, through unstructured situations like communicating orally and reading casually without direct instruction, as well as routine teacher modeling.

Closed-captioned and subtitled TV and movies

Closed-captioning originally was designed to facilitate TV and movie viewing by deaf and hard-of-hearing persons. However, once this technology was available widely, it became popular with many hearing users, and has been found educationally valuable for diverse students. Federal law has mandated built-in closed-captioning on every TV set since 1993; today, movies, sports events, live news broadcasts, most TV programs, and also many online videos include closed-captions. Research studies find that students with learning disabilities (LD), those with other academic difficulties, and those learning English as a non-native language can all benefit from classroom videos that include captions. Captioned/subtitled media can support teachers in providing differentiated instruction in classrooms. Beginning readers, struggling readers, and LD students can realize improvements in word recognition, vocabulary knowledge and acquisition, decoding skills, reading comprehension, silent reading speed, and oral reading speed. Studies find viewing video improves comprehension skills, and watching captioned video enhances vocabulary learning. Even beginning readers can benefit from captioned videos with simpler vocabularies.

Research has found that students learning English as a new language gain greater enhancement in overall listening comprehension from watching captioned videos than non-captioned videos. Also, native English-speaking students who view captioned videos in learning foreign languages demonstrate improved listening comprehension, reading comprehension, word recognition, decoding skills, new vocabulary learning, and motivation. Studies also find using multimedia in foreign-language instruction can decrease student anxiety about not knowing the language, and increase their motivation to learn it. Moreover, even in other studies not showing significant academic improvements, students still report preferences for captioned over non-captioned video. Therefore, captioned media can additionally improve students' non-academic skills like motivation, time-on-task, and classroom behavior by increasing their enjoyment in reading activities. Researchers find reading captions relatively intuitive, needing little added student instruction/training. Even beginning/struggling readers typically try to decode caption text. Furthermore, captioning alters watching videos from predominantly picture-viewing to predominantly reading activities, supporting reading instruction with more print exposure and reading practice. Parents' using TV captions at home can greatly increase these.

Impact of reading skills on student success

The ability to read is not simply one academic area; it is a basic skill set underlying all academic activity, and determines whether students fail or succeed in school. Research shows that of first-graders with poor reading skills, 88% still read poorly in fourth grade. By this time, most information that students require is provided in text form. For this reason, the focus shifts from learning to read in the earlier grades, to reading to learn by fourth grade. Consequently, students with poor reading skills can find it harder to access and interact with the content in their schools' curricula. Moreover, reading abilities that are delayed or disordered usually are identified in higher elementary grades. Yet research finds remediation attempts then could be too late, because children acquire language and have literacy experiences from birth. Phonemic awareness, the alphabetic principle, and print awareness normally develop in early childhood. Children missing such early experiences will fall behind peers without extra instruction. This means elementary school teachers must give these children literacy-rich environments.

Skill areas that are necessary for children to develop literacy

According to studies by the National Reading Panel, for children to develop literacy, they must have developed skills in phonemic awareness, phonics, vocabulary, comprehension, and fluency. A prerequisite to developing these five skill areas is having an understanding of how literacy works, what it does, and how it is used. While young children exposed to spoken and printed language interactions from birth often develop this understanding of the functions and applications of literacy in a natural way, children with language and learning disabilities may not. A literacy-rich environment is defined as one that provides students having disabilities with stimulation to take part in activities involving language and literacy during their everyday life routines. Stimulating such participation in and integration of language and literacy into daily living is an effective way to help disabled students begin to develop understanding of how spoken and printed language function and are used. Teaching strategies to establish literacy-rich environments can not only remediate language and literacy deficits, but also benefit all elementary-level students.

Literacy-rich environment

An elementary classroom constituting a literacy-rich setting would engage all students in various literacy activities, some working individually and others in groups. Students would explore different genres of books, not only during reading periods or in the library, but during math, social studies, and science periods or lessons. The teacher might read aloud to students from a book about math during math period, and lead class discussions of the book's content, and have students explore eyewitness science books during science time to learn about scientific concepts. These activities help students experience literacy across all curriculum subject content areas. Students also use books on tapes and CD-ROMs. The classroom includes adapted materials to motivate disabled students to read and help them interact with text. Students write in notebooks and journals, write reports in all subjects, and compose books. A literacy-rich classroom environment features information resources for students including dictionaries, encyclopedias, books in varied genres, word walls, and computers, as well as teachers and peers.

Literacy across the curriculum for students with and without disabilities

In a classroom that supports literacy, the teacher should provide labels combining words and pictures on all objects. This continually stimulates students to associate written language with the objects and concepts it represents. Especially to support disabled students, teachers should use their particular interests and needs as a guide for labeling things. Printed directions, signs, calendars, and schedules are materials that students should use regularly in the classroom. These help students realize how language is used in everyday life. When the class is studying a certain topic, theme, or book, the teacher and students can work together to redesign the classroom using printed/written materials that reflect that topic, theme, or book. This enables students to experience fully and "live" the lesson rather than just observing it. All of the materials must be adapted for any students' special needs. For instance, in a class including blind/visually impaired students, labels, signs and other print materials can incorporate Braille words and textured surfaces.

Addressing diverse student abilities and needs

Teachers must consider the diversity among the skills and needs of their students as they design their classroom learning environments. The teachers should individualize the setting and their instruction so that these represent every student. Individualization and instructional differentiation should not only address disabled students' needs; they should also regularly provide suitable opportunities for these students to participate on an ongoing basis in activities that involve literacy and integrate it into all content areas. According to research, a salient need of students with diverse literacy backgrounds is that they often have trouble connecting new information to their existing knowledge. This ability is a critical component of learning. When teachers plan and organize their classrooms to offer literacy activities that are accessible to disabled students—and that immerse them in literacy experiences and give them opportunities to connect both new with old information, and spoken with printed language—these students can then access the general education curriculum.

Helping students with disabilities develop literacy skills

To participate in the general curriculum, students with disabilities need to understand the alphabetic principle, i.e. that printed language represents spoken language; connect print with speech; and be able to relate new information to their prior knowledge. Teachers can support these developments by designing classrooms as literacy-rich settings, immersing special-needs and other students in accessible literacy activities across all content areas. For example, students can interact with alphabet-letter magnets, cookie-cutters, and stamps: concrete manipulatives allow students not developmentally ready for exclusively abstract thought to understand concepts using real objects. Discussing daily schedules requires students to read and comprehend printed language, and then use spoken language to demonstrate and apply their understanding. Playing letter/word games like Bingo, Pictionary, Boggle, and Scrabble gives practice with creating and manipulating language, enhancing recognition and cognitive flexibility. Providing photos of peers, teachers, staff, and classroom activities and having students label them helps students connect written language with familiar, meaningful images. Daily communication notebooks help students further integrate literacy into their school days.

Classrooms with multicultural backgrounds

Implications regarding literacy development for classroom teachers with students from multicultural backgrounds

Educational research shows that the cultural values of families and/or communities influence children's literacy development, and also that culture is a significant factor to understanding children's home literacy environments. Researchers have also found that cultural purposes, perspectives, and contexts affect how students with disabilities in particular interact with the literacy environments they encounter. They say children's preparation levels entering formal education reflect their families'/communities' values and beliefs about literacy. Cultural attitudes about literacy then influence how schools deliver instruction and literacy experiences. Teachers must assess culturally diverse students' interactions with the environment, and design literacy-rich classrooms, with students' diverse backgrounds in mind. Students learning English (ELL/ESL) enter school either not knowing English; or just learning it, lacking exposure to specific vocabulary and literature. Literacy-rich classrooms help them participate in regular curriculum. Teacher should read aloud often to these students; include print in their native language in classrooms; permit mistakes during student attempts to use English; encourage students to reread books repeatedly; and plan activities entailing language use.

Whole-class vs. traditional small-group classroom

A major disadvantage of whole-class reading is that students who read above the average class level go unchallenged and can become bored, while students reading below average level are lost. Yet the small-group method intended to remedy this also has the drawback that, as traditionally implemented, most time is used for skill instruction, leaving far too little time for students actually to read the text. One solution is a flexible grouping model, e.g., Grouping Without Tracking (Paratore, 1990). This model uses a "sandwich" structure: teachers give students shared-reading processes at the beginning and end of the lesson, but provide differentiated instruction to two groups in the middle as they read the text. Teachers give indirect guidance to students who can read more independently, and more direct support to struggling readers. Teachers reunite the groups to lead them in a final discussion. Students with reading difficulties gain reading proficiency and comprehension from direct teacher support, enabling them to contribute better to the whole-class discussion, so all share this experience equally.

Jigsaw approach to shared reading

Students reading below grade level may be able to access and comprehend some texts or portions of them, but have difficulty with harder parts/texts—for example, informational texts with more challenging subject matter and specialized vocabulary. When a text intended for the whole class contains such challenging material, one solution the teacher can use is a jigsaw approach. The teacher selects various portions of the text that are less difficult and assigns them to students reading below grade level. Whereas such texts overall might present struggles for these students, they find the easier portions more manageable when they tackle only these parts, as selected and assigned by the teacher, in small groups of students with comparable reading levels. The teacher makes each small student group responsible for comprehension of their assigned portion of text. Then the teacher brings the class back together, having each group report what they read, understood, and learned. The whole class then collaborates to help each other make connections among the learning each group reported.

Texts used for reading exercises

Any inclusive classroom will contain students who read at various age/grade levels. As a result, some books used as core texts are going to present difficulties for some of the students, who read below grade level and/or lack background knowledge and vocabulary of the subject. One way a teacher can facilitate all students' comprehension of such texts is to provide supplementary texts that allow readers at different levels easier access—texts on the same subject or theme as the more difficult core text. Teachers have students read these more accessible texts independently during small-group reading periods. This makes it easier for students with less reading proficiency to learn the core vocabulary and build their background knowledge. Thus they are more prepared to tackle the more difficult core text during whole-class shared reading periods. With such preparation, less proficient readers are more likely to become engaged and active participants in the shared reading of a difficult text in the whole-group setting.

Assigning students to small groups for guided reading exercises

Expert educators and researchers recommend that when teachers divide classes into small student groups for guided reading, they should not be overly concerned with assigning students to exact reading levels. Rather, though they will want to group students whose literacy development is similar and who read *around* a similar level, they should give more attention to organizing groups according to the students' areas of need. For example, a teacher might identify students who share in common a need for help with noticing changes in setting; other students who share difficulties with recognizing and differentiating characters; some students who demonstrate problems with following and/or reproducing events they read in a text in the correct chronological sequence; some students who have trouble identifying and/or articulating the main idea in a text portion, etc. The teacher can create a group of students sharing one of these challenges; announce to the class what this group's focus is; and then invite other students to join this group by choice if they experience the same need.

Making word counts

Books designed for lower reading levels typically contain fewer words, both per page and overall. Yet students who are reading below their grade levels require not fewer reading opportunities, but more, to practice and improve their reading skills. For example, within one class of second-grade students, the teacher might have one group using a text with over 80 words on just the first page, while another group uses a text with a total of 80 words in the entire book. This difference shows that the teacher will need to use several texts within certain groups to give them equal amounts of reading material and practice as readers of denser/longer texts during group reading times. Teachers can look at the backs of the books they assign during guided reading sessions, and maintain simple logs of their word counts. Comparing these word counts among groups can help teachers to equalize the numbers of words that each student group actually works with during small-group guided reading periods.

Connecting text sets

When teachers select textbooks to teach a unit/lesson on a certain topic, they often compile text sets—groups of books all related to the same topic/theme. Because classes are usually include students reading at different levels, teachers also often gather books at different reading levels for text sets. When collecting books representing multiple reading levels, the teacher can also intentionally organize the text set so all books are connected. For example, the books might share similar content; similar language, style, and vocabulary words; or similar layouts. Selecting books sharing such a commonality at different reading levels makes it easier for students to draw useful connections between easier and harder texts. It also facilitates students' flexibility in working across multiple reading levels, which builds their skills and confidence for faster progress. Additionally, to prepare some students to read books that teachers felt would prove too difficult otherwise, they can use easier texts with similar themes/language/formats to establish contexts for the harder ones.

Enhancing students' independent reading

In addition to whole-class and small-group reading exercises, students need some time reading texts of their own choice, which they can easily read with little/no support, to attain comfort, fluency, and confidence. To ensure more opportunities for practice, with equal time for all students, teachers should provide text sets at multiple reading levels for each content area. Experts suggest 70% of books should be easily accessible; and, in addition to classroom libraries, using rolling carts lets book collections travel among classrooms. Multiple reading levels let more advanced readers peruse a harder text, while less advanced readers read several easier texts; this equalizes the time and words they have for practicing. Because critics find some leveled readers lack variety in gender/race/class/other sociocultural aspects of characters, teachers should build diverse book collections representing all students. Teachers can inform their selections via student interest surveys; and familiarity with students' individual identities, personalities, and special interests. Knowing individual students can help match them to texts as effectively as leveled book lists.

Engaging students in reading

Experts find excessive attention to leveling as a way of matching texts to students can be restrictive, undermining high-quality instruction that balances the needs of the reader with the demands of the text. Teachers must consider that assigning certain texts will cause students to disengage from reading and avoid it rather than engage in it. In the real world, people read many different kinds of materials. Therefore, a teacher has better chances of finding texts that engage students, and that motivate them to read and allow them to perceive themselves as readers, by mindfully selecting varied text genres with varied difficulty. In classrooms incorporating various student reading levels, this can be the best method to procure classroom acceptability of accessible texts. Teachers can also use individualized instructional formats, such as Readers Workshop (Atwell, 1998), which balance issues of difficulty, choice, and engagement; develop reader communities affording more reading experiences with authenticity, meaning, and enjoyment; and stronger positive teacher-student relationships via individualized consultations. Teachers should also incorporate accessible alternative texts for independent activities.

Alternative reading and writing forms

When students read and write outside of school, they choose many alternative forms of reading and writing. To engage these students while they are in school, teachers should think about adding such alternative materials to their own instructional programs. For example, teachers might incorporate such media as graphic novels, magazines, newspapers, plays, anthologies of poetry, e-books and other digital/online content, and text that students have written themselves. Educational experts advise that just because it can be harder to determine the reading levels of such alternative text formats, teachers should not shy away from using them. Because they represent examples of text that people (including students) read in real life, they provide not only excellent practice for students' present and future reading of real-world materials, but also motivation to read and meaningful experiences in reading. Another boon of using these authentic, alternative texts is that they frequently incorporate multiple reading levels, so that nearly every student can read some portions of them.

Copyright © Mometrix Media. You have been licensed one copy of this document for personal use only. Any other reproduction or redistribution is strictly prohibited. All rights reserved.

Safe and respectful learning environments

Educational researchers have surveyed school principals, asking them to identify what they believe are the most important staff development topics related to school safety. For example, principals asked about these topics in 2000 responded that they found systems for behavior management; in-school programs aimed at prevention of bullying and other harm at the primary level; how to address inappropriate behavior; training in implementing emergency procedures; and academics as the most important staff development areas. When asked what they found the most important obstacle they faced in ensuring safe school environments, more than half of principals identified the lack of resources. Researchers also found that principals expressed significant concern about episodes of bullying, harassment, and mean-spirited teasing in their schools. In addition to principals, among the students themselves, surveyors received reports from close to 40% of high school students across the country that mean-spirited teasing, harassment, and bullying have negative impacts on school attendance, peer relationships, and academic achievement.

With regard to how schools are regulated, the majority of educational researchers find certain characteristics in schools are associated with more discipline problems. For example, when school rules are not clear; are stated but not enforced consistently; students do not find the rules important; or administrators and teachers do not have a clear sense of how to interpret and/or enforce rules; these conditions contribute to issues with discipline. Additionally, if school administrators and teachers fail to cooperate with school rules; administrators fail to engage or take action; the teachers exhibit punitive attitudes; and/or teachers and administrators ignore student misbehavior, discipline becomes problematic. Schools with insufficient teaching resources, and larger schools, are also at risk for discipline problems. Studies show that in schools whose behavior management is most effective, the school rules are clear and are communicated to all school community members; the principals are active, highly visible, communicate clearly with the staff and students, and personally monitor problem areas; and the school's atmosphere promotes treating students as individuals.

A number of initiatives by state school boards and educational researchers show interest in exploring whether students' engagement in schools and academic settings can be increased via strategies of integrating civil discourse. The majority of U.S. states collect data to quantify how effective schools are. These data include such variables as how students are performing on large-scale, high-stakes achievement tests; what kinds of courses students are completing; rates of graduation among high school students; the comparative quality of post-graduate options for their students; and also how effectively a school fosters a safe learning environment. In most U.S. states, data on rates of expulsion, suspension, and disciplinary referrals of students are gathered as indices of how well the schools do at creating environments where students feel safe, respected, and able to learn. Some state boards of education direct local school districts to develop standards for civil interactions among all school community members; and boards of education to hold public hearings seeking student and community input for defining such standards and policies.

Public opinion and school policies

When U.S. state educational initiatives conduct research to survey the public about school district policies, they often find that the majority of the population view schools as having important roles in helping students develop positive values. For example, in Oregon, a statewide public opinion poll yielded 77% of responses that schools should help students develop "good values;" and 78% gave high ratings to the role of schools for helping students to develop strong work ethics. In addition, citizens responded to surveys that they agreed strongly with the idea of school districts adopting policies that require each school building to establish a written plan for producing greater civility and a more positive climate for learning. Proponents of such policies feel that school boards should adopt standards regarding the dress, language, and interactions among all members of the school community; and that all school districts should not only implement policies for civility, but should also report the standards resulting from such policies to their state departments and boards of education.

For schools to create learning environments where students feel safe and respected, many state boards of education have recommended that their local school districts should extend their existing standards for student conduct and discipline to incorporate civility standards and plans. State officials advise that all parents and children should understand and agree to such rules. Moreover, the idea of school civility standards applies to all people on school grounds, and all members of the school community. This includes students, teachers, parents, volunteers, administrators, non-teaching staff, and visitors to the schools. All of these people must be treated and treat others civilly and with respect. This enables students to learn, and teaches them values of civility and respect. Experts find that school civility policies achieve three main results: (1) they promote a safe environment for learning; (2) they supply students with models for appropriate civil discourse and for problem-solving processes; and (3) they limit the rates of violent episodes occurring in the schools.

Intrinsic and extrinsic motivation

In addition to contextual support such as explicit instruction by teachers and their provision of suitable texts to students for promoting reading proficiency, motivational support is also important. When students read something, they most often have some reason for reading. When students read without being assigned to read, the most common reason they give for reading is that they enjoy it. Reading for interest is an example of intrinsic motivation to read: the student's reason comes from internal factors. Students who read for the sake of reading typically demonstrate high reading achievement. Researchers have found that students reading from intrinsic motivation spend triple the time reading than those with low internal motivation. And intrinsic motivation correlates more highly than other motivations with frequent, wide, independent reading by students. Extrinsic motivation is from outside sources, such as because the teacher assigned it, and/or to avoid getting in trouble. Because this is not by the student's choice, students tend to avoid reading from external motivations that do not correlate with reading achievement.

Research finds students who read by their own choice, out of interest and/or for enjoyment, have intrinsic/internal motivation to read and are typically high-achieving readers; while students who read because their teacher assigned it, to avoid getting into trouble for not doing it, or for external rewards (e.g. food/toys/grades) have extrinsic/external motivation, which is not correlated with high reading achievement. With elementary-school, student research does not typically find negative correlations between external motivations for reading and reading proficiency. In other words, external reasons to read seem not to harm younger students' reading competence. This may be because children at earlier developmental levels for behavior and self-regulation usually need some external inducements to engage in an emerging behavior like reading. However, research finds that high-school students who read only from external motivations exhibit declining and low achievement in reading. For this reason, interest in reading is critical for secondary-school students to develop reading competence and quality. Intrinsic motivation and interest enable high-school students' deep interaction with text and attainment of greater knowledge.

Motivational factors promoting reading achievement

Educational researchers find that student reading achievement is promoted by student: (1) interest in reading; (2) ownership, meaning the student feels s/he has some choice in the reading and the reading belongs to him/her; (3) self-efficacy, i.e., the student feels a sense of his/her own competence to perform the reading/reading-related tasks; (4) social interaction that students engage in related to reading, such as comprehending, discussing, and analyzing the text, and collaborating on assigned projects based on the reading; and (5) mastery, meaning the student feels s/he has mastered the skills required to read with comprehension, richness, breadth, and depth. Motivational programs for reading instruction, like Concept-Oriented Reading Instruction (CORI), focus not only on helping students to achieve reading comprehension, but also on helping students at all reading levels to become engaged in reading. For example, CORI trains teachers in five motivational practices corresponding to the five motivational factors listed above. These motivational practices are also integrated into the curriculum. Research studies have validated the effectiveness of these motivational practices.

Student motivation

Enhancing corresponding student motivation
(1) When teachers select reading matter that is **relevant** to students, this provides them with *intrinsic/internal motivation and interest* to read. When reading material is relevant and interests students, their reasons to read are: they enjoy it; it is fun. (2) When teachers allow students **choice**—e.g., among texts, topics, assessment methods, activity sequences, etc.—they experience *ownership* of reading; their reasons to read are: they chose it; it belongs to them. (3) When teachers arrange for students to experience **success** in reading, they experience *self-efficacy*, i.e., they are competent to perform the tasks. Their reasons to read are: they can read well; they like succeeding. (4) When teachers arrange for student **collaboration** in reading-related activities, this provides *social peer interaction*. Their reasons for reading are: they can read with their peers; they enjoy relating to classmates. (5) When teachers present **thematic units** for reading, students experience *mastery*; their reasons to read are: they want to understand; they like learning new things.

Practices discouraging student motivation
(1) When teachers provide reading materials that are **not relevant** to students, the outcome is they *avoid* reading, for the reasons that: they do not enjoy it; it is not fun. (2) When teachers exert **excessive control** over student reading, students experience *low ownership*. They avoid reading because: it was not their choice; they do not feel it belongs to them. (3) When teachers give overly **difficult lessons**, students experience greater *perceived difficulty* in reading. Their reasons to avoid reading are: they cannot accomplish it; they do not feel competent. (4) When teachers assign only **individual work** too often, the outcome for students is feeling *isolation*. They avoid reading because: they cannot read with other students; they feel unable to relate to their peers around reading. (5) When teachers present **disconnected units**, not thematically related reading, the outcome is that students

avoid mastery. Their reasons to avoid reading are: they cannot construct meaning from the text; and they do not care about their reading comprehension.

<u>Evidence-based teacher practices that encourage student motivation</u>
Studies recognize that motivation is an essential factor to reading success, and identify five practical ways for teachers to enhance student motivation to read: to "honor" books for students then to select on their own; to read aloud to students; to establish balanced book collections; to publicize students' reading passions; and to provide incentives or rewards that affirm the value of reading. Research finds that when teachers do anything to single out a book as "special," even as simply as standing the book up on a table, children will select that book over others. Teachers can pick out individual books to feature in displays, and/or to include in book baskets, to highlight them for student attention. A teacher can show a book to the class; read a few pages to them; and/or ask them questions about the book to pique their interest in it. Such introductions often stimulate students' desire to find out what is contained in the books, making books introduced this way very popular with students.

Reading books aloud

Reading aloud daily enables teachers to share book orally with students, with the purposes of modeling reading strategies and behaviors for students and stimulating instructional discussions. Multiple child development theories find that the socialization involved in read-alouds permits teachers and students to collaborate in constructing meaning from the text. Teachers should read a broad variety of texts aloud to students, including informational books, magazines, and newspapers. During read-alouds, teachers should encourage interaction with students by starting discussions. The give-and-take of conversations about a shared text involves students in thinking, reasoning, and making inferences and predictions, developing their higher cognitive skills. When teachers periodically ask students to choose the read-aloud text, such as offering several titles to select from and letting students vote, students feel greater text ownership through having a choice. Teachers can also let students read text of their choice aloud sometimes, including advance rehearsal, to enhance all students' motivation.

Building a balanced collection of books

Researchers and educators generally agree it is important to expose young students to a balanced variety of reading materials. The International Reading Association maintains that children should be exposed to a variety of book genres. These include, for example, picture storybooks; fiction; nonfiction; poetry; and magazines. Some expert tips for teachers to balance their book collections include: Teachers should incorporate a broadly diverse selection of informational books, both in their reading instruction in their classroom libraries. Teachers should accept student reading and learning from fictional and nonfictional books, newspapers, magazines, and electronic books. Teachers should celebrate their students as authors by "publishing" their writing in their classrooms' libraries and/or "news corners." Student works should reflect class diversity. They may include nonverbal picture books, puzzle books, fictional stories, poetry, comic books/graphic novels, how-to guidebooks, informational books, photo documentaries, recipe books, journals, news articles, and postcard collections. Teachers should also engage students in choosing books for the classroom library and/or school library through reviewing, discussing, debating, and voting on possible book choices.

Publicizing students' reading passions

Young children typically have high curiosity about books with which they feel familiar. Curiosity motivates children to read. Regarding books they enjoy reading most, children often report interest in a book because they had read other books in the series/about the character, knew/knew about the author, or heard about it from friends. Teachers can publicize students' reading passions by making a "Wall of Fame" on a bulletin board that they continually update and change to reflect student interests. The display may include favorite books, series, magazines etc., of students, teachers, families, and principals. Also, "Top 10" lists are very popular (for example, they are regularly featured and enjoyed on *The Late Show with David Letterman*). Teachers can have students vote and publish the classroom's Top 10 reading list periodically. They can make this a school-year-long activity by making separate lists of the top 10 informational books, fictional books, poems, magazines, and websites. Teachers can include small-group discussions for students to share their reading passions as part of self-selected reading periods.

Incentives and rewards

In reading programs that allow incentives for students, educational experts recommend that teachers think about offering students rewards for reading that are themselves closely related to reading. The significance of such rewards related to reading extends past the behavioral principle of the reward's immediacy following the targeted behavior. Experts speculate that a classroom culture that is nurturing and supportive of internal motivations for reading is reflected both in the desired behavior of reading, and in the rewards for reading, which also involve reading themselves. For example, rewards that teachers offer students for reading, which also confirm the inherent value of reading, can include: giving students books; giving students more time for read-aloud activities; giving students more time for reading self-selected materials; giving students more time to spend in and using the library; providing more frequent and regular times for students to talk about books with others; and the establishment and participation in book clubs for students.

Application of Theoretical and Knowledge Bases of Reading in Diagnosis and Assessment

Nature and prevalence of reading difficulties

Young students' difficulties with reading are not characterized as existent vs. nonexistent, but rather along a continuum. This means that a broad range of students experience some kinds of reading problems. Some students have diagnoses of learning disabilities (LD) that interfere with reading easily. Even larger numbers of others are not diagnosed with LD, but nevertheless need instructional help targeting the specific problems they encounter with reading. Some experts estimate that approximately ten million children experience trouble with learning to read. However, they also find that of children with reading impairments, approximately 90-95% can surmount these problems if they are given suitable intervention at young ages. Adults should not rely on formal diagnoses as signs of reading problems; they must watch for children's progress and/or problems. Adults must first (1) ascertain accurately the type and cause of a child's reading problem; (2) give instruction targeting problem remediation and skills improvement; and (3) make accommodations for student needs and build on student strengths.

Reading problems

Indications of reading problem
Parents, caregivers, and teachers should attend to how each individual child is progressing in skills areas prerequisite and related to reading. For example, with preschool-aged children, adults should observe whether a child has comparatively more difficulty than his/her age peers with pronouncing words, learning the alphabet, recognizing and producing rhymes; learning colors and/or shapes of concrete objects; learning numbers; and/or learning the days of the week. Adults can also consult many sources available online and on paper that identify common developmental milestones in language development and reading development. If a child regularly demonstrates difficulty with several developmental milestones, the adult(s) should consider having the child evaluated for potential reading and/or learning disabilities. Adults should keep in mind that children learn at different rates and in different ways. However, the majority of students with normal development can read grade-level materials, with comprehension and fluency, by the end of third grade. Preventing students from falling behind grade level in reading is important, because reading problems are best remediated at early ages.

Probability to develop reading problems
While any student can have reading problems for a variety of causes, some students have higher probabilities of encountering difficulty with reading. Adults need to know about these relationships, as their knowledge can inform their monitoring of students at higher risk for deficits in reading skills. Closer monitoring enables earlier detection of problems and intervention to address them. For example, children of parents who have histories of reading problems can be more likely also to present with reading problems. Children with hearing impairments have a higher likelihood of reading problems, since the normal basis for language and reading development is auditory. Children with visual impairments are

also more likely to have delays and/or deficits in visually reading print. Children who have received diagnoses of specific language impairments have a greater probability of reading problems, as do students with cognitive disabilities. In addition, children without physical or cognitive deficits who were exposed less to literacy-related knowledge and/or skills during their preschool development are found more likely to develop reading difficulties.

Findings about the nature of reading problems

Researchers find the main occurrence of reading difficulties is at the single-word level. One must be able to separate words and syllables into individual phonemes (speech sounds) and recognize the letters representing these to decode printed words. People who struggle with reading, of all ages as well as all intelligence and socioeconomic levels, commonly share decoding difficulties. In Western languages, the printed language code is alphabetic; even printed Eastern languages (like Chinese) that are ideographic/logographic also encode speech sounds. Therefore, when a child masters the relationship between print and linguistic sound structures, s/he has developed decoding ability. But the student must additionally develop speed and accuracy in decoding to do it efficiently. Such decoding efficiency frees up the reader's processes of attention and memory to apply to reading comprehension. While most children develop decoding proficiency regardless of instructional methods, about 30% do not, requiring teaching. Research finds systematic, direct instruction in the alphabetic code most effective to develop early literacy and combat illiteracy.

Factors that cause reading problems

(1) Neurological factors: Science finds the brain metabolisms of good vs. poor readers differ while processing word sounds, such as identifying whether they rhyme. Researchers believe this is related more to brain function than structure. Recent neuropsychological studies suggest brain functions may improve via improving reading skills through neuroplasticity, the brain's ability to change and adapt. (2) Familial factors: Reading difficulties run in families; however, genetic components interact with environmental influences. For instance, adults with poor reading skills are less likely to read to their children than adults with good reading skills. Instruction is crucial for children with poor reading in their family histories. (3) Social/cultural factors: Parental literacy, early exposure of children to print, and parental reading to children vary with social/cultural characteristics. Their effects are somewhat inflated due to the high effectiveness of research interventions with socioeconomically disadvantaged groups. (4) Instructional factors: These can be undervalued in that literacy skills can be taught in grades P/K-2. Many children need explicit instruction in literacy skills for several years.

Reading difficulties vs. reading disabilities

Some students are not formally diagnosed with any reading or learning disability, but nevertheless struggle to read. Some such children simply progress a bit slower than their age peers. Some may need more time for learning certain concepts/skills. Some might have had prior reading instruction that was inadequate. Others might need reading instruction that is more specialized than what they have received. Regardless, students with reading difficulties need informed attention from parents, schools, and teachers to improve their reading skills. Students who do have formal diagnoses of learning disabilities (LD) are entitled to receive special education services by the federal Individuals with Disabilities Education Act (IDEA). This law also mandates that every student with a disability have an Individualized Education Program (IEP) developed for him/her. Support and services related to reading can be part of the IEP goals and objectives. Research finds that reading disabilities probably exist in at least 20% of the US population; yet among school-aged students, only around 4% receive special education services for them.

Learning disability (LD)

Students who experience learning disabilities have more difficulty than is normal in learning certain kinds of skills or specific academic content areas. Learning disabilities have no relationship to levels of intelligence. Neuropsychologists have discovered that frequently, individuals with LDs have physiological differences in the ways that their brains are "wired." These differences do not mean that they are less or more intelligent, or that their cognitive processes are worse or better than those of others. However, researchers find that as many as 80% of learning disabilities are manifested as difficulties with learning to read. Diagnosticians often describe ongoing problems with learning to read as dyslexia, which encompasses a wide variety of difficulties with the reading process. Deficits in auditory language processing, which interfere with fluently and accurately reading words, are often found to cause dyslexia. This lack of fluency and accuracy in reading can then cause students to experience difficulties with their reading comprehension as well.

Studies investigating reading difficulties find that these exist along a continuum of reading ability; therefore, the causes of poor reading and good reading are the same. Research has identified that at least 10 million of American children read poorly. Studies show that boys and girls experience reading problems at equivalent rates; however, schools identify boys with reading problems four times more than girls. This is mostly due to behavioral factors rather than differences in learning. The identification of school-aged children with reading problems has greatly increased over time: special education statistics show that before 1980, fewer than 25% of children in special education programs were identified with learning disabilities, while more than 50% were identified with LDs by 1993. Out of all children in schools identified with LDs, 80% have primarily reading problems; of this group, 90% have difficulties specifically with developing decoding skills, which are necessary for reading fluently and with comprehension.

Much research has found that the earlier a child's age when intervention begins to improve reading skills, the more effective that intervention is. However, even when reading problems have been detected early in a child's life, some adults may sometimes assume that over time, the child will "grow out" of these difficulties. Although even normally developing children progress at a variety of rates, numerous studies have demonstrated that among children who read poorly in third grade, almost ¾ of them are still reading poorly when they have reached ninth grade. The single most common source of reading difficulty is poor skills in decoding the relationships of letters to sounds. Some adults may also assume that students can overcome decoding deficiencies by context, through overall reading comprehension; however, reading comprehension is dependent on decoding skills, among others. The strongest predictor of inadequate reading comprehension is incorrect and slow decoding. Although poor reading has many causes, its characteristic decoding difficulties are primarily at the single-word level.

Requirements for a student to learn to read

(1) Phonological awareness is recognizing the sound structures of spoken language, not just the meanings it conveys. This is a reading prerequisite. (2) Phonemic awareness is the skill

of recognizing and manipulating individual speech sounds or phonemes. Students must be able to segment words and syllables into phonemes to learn to read. (3) The Alphabetic Principle is the concept that printed language consists of alphabet letters that are deliberately and systematically related to the individual sounds of spoken language. Reading depends on understanding this concept. (4) Orthographic awareness is recognition of printed language structures, such as orthographic rules, patterns in spelling; derivational morphology and inflectional morphology, i.e. structural changes indicating word types and grammatical differences; and etymology, i.e. word and meaning origins. Efficient reading requires orthographic awareness. (5) Comprehensive monitoring strategies: Students need full repertoires of techniques that will help them to attend to and retain the information that they read.

Fundamental skills that students must know

To become good readers, students must have phonological awareness, i.e. knowing the structures of speech sounds. They must understand the alphabetic principle, i.e. that alphabet letters represent specific speech sounds in print and writing. They must have orthographic awareness, i.e. knowing the rules, structures, and patterns in the spelling and grammar of written/printed language. And they must have acquired multiple and varied strategies to support their reading comprehension and retention. Teachers must be educated and prepared in linguistics, psycholinguistics, and reading; in how to assess and diagnose student skills in reading and spelling; and in a thorough complement of strategies for conducting reading interventions. Teachers need to instruct their students in such concepts and skills as segmenting words/syllables; alliteration; rhyming; phonics patterns and their representation in text; conventions of spelling and writing; being able to identify the main idea in text; being able to draw inferences from reading; and a wide range of study skills to help students comprehend, remember, and apply what they read.

Instructional interventions

According to all of the research by the National Institute of Child Health and Human Development (NICHD), teaching approaches that embed literacy or emphasize context are not as effective for developing reading skills as direct instruction in alphabetic decoding skills. Within this type of instruction, the kind of individual program used matters less than teacher training and monitoring; the duration and intensity of the program; and the program's being explicit and structured. Studies also find that among children beginning first grade who read below the 15th percentile, more than 90A% will read at grade level or above by the end of the school year when they receive suitable interventions. Moreover, a study by the University of Houston found when a regular kindergarten curriculum incorporated 15 minutes daily teaching the alphabetic code, children made significant improvements in phonological analysis skills compared to children receiving the same curriculum without this addition. Researchers also found this instruction had to continue in the following school years for students' reading ability to benefit.

Instructional approaches

When researchers compared instructional approaches emphasizing context, those using embedded phonics, and those explicitly teaching phonics to first- and second-grade students receiving Title 1 services for socially disadvantaged populations, they found after intervention for one school year, the only approach achieving average reading proficiency levels was direct instruction. They even found no improvements for many children taught using context-based approaches. They concluded the influence of curriculum was stronger than the influences of different teachers and of tutoring. Studies also find that while students require skills in phonological analysis and decoding to read successfully, these alone are insufficient. Students must additionally develop the ability for rapid decoding of words that demonstrate the orthographic components of our language, such as morphological units (the smallest grammatical units conveying different meanings) and writing conventions. Students must also be taught individual comprehension processes. Reading skills are affected by literacy immersion, print awareness, and being read to, but do not predict long-term reading success as strongly as single-word skills.

Norm-referenced test

Norm-referenced tests are formal assessment instruments that compare a student's performance to that of a sample representative of the general population of the child's age/grade peers in responding to a set of standardized items. The range of scores achieved by students in the sample is considered average or normal; for this reason, these scores are considered the norm. Comparing each student's test scores to this norm gives educators and parents an idea how a student's school achievement measures up with reference to the norm—hence the term "norm-referenced test." Some norm-referenced tests that are commonly used in public school systems include the Stanford-Binet and Wechsler tests—the Wechsler Preschool and Primary Scales of Intelligence (WPPSI), Wechsler Intelligence Scales for Children (WISC), and for students aged 16+, the Wechsler Adult Intelligence Scales (WAIS)—for assessing intelligence; the Iowa Test of Basic Skills (ITBS); and the Wechsler Individual Achievement Test (WIAT) and Woodcock-Johnson tests, which are often used to monitor student progress in school.

Criterion-referenced test

Norm-referenced and criterion-referenced tests are typically both standardized. However, whereas a norm-referenced test is an assessment tool that compares a student's results to those of other students in the same age/grade group to define how that student performs relative to an established norm, a criterion-referenced test does not measure a student's performance compared to those of his/her peer group. Rather, it measures a student's performance compared to standardized established criteria. In addition to these criteria, assessments using criterion-referenced tests may also compare the student's current performance on a test to the same student's previous performance on the same test as a means of evaluating the student's progress in school. A few examples of criterion-referenced tests used to monitor student progress include the Texas Primary Reading Inventory (TEA, 2000), the Academic Intervention Monitoring System (AIMS; Elliott et al, 2001), and the Academic Competence Evaluation Systems (ACES; DiPerna & Elliott, 2000).

Informal reading assessment

To assess a student's awareness of print concepts 1:1, a teacher should arrange for a quiet, comfortable setting without distractions. Ideally, another teacher or aide can supervise the class in working quietly while the assessing teacher sits in a quiet corner with one student. The teacher should have a simple checklist, with each task listed and Yes/No columns to check for each task the student can/cannot complete successfully. Teachers can complete this checklist several times per school year, periodically repeating tasks the student did not succeed at until s/he can do so. The teacher gives the student a storybook and asks him/her to demonstrate the following: Recognize the book's front; recognize the book's back; identify the book's title; identify a word on/in the book; identify a letter in a word in the book; identify a space between words in the book; identify the place where the teacher should start reading the book aloud; and identify a period as the punctuation mark ending a sentence.

When informally assessing a child's ability to identify rhymes, the teacher first asks the child whether s/he knows what rhyming words are. If the child answers "Yes," the teacher then asks the child to supply two words that rhyme. If the child answers "No," or says "Yes" but gives a non-rhyming example, the teacher explains that rhyming words end with the same sound and gives an example, like *hat* and *cat.* The teacher tells the student, "I'm going to say two words; I want you to tell me if they sound the same at the end." The teacher uses a simple checklist. Each item will list the two words presented, with places for Correct or Incorrect to check or circle indicating the child's answer. The actual word pairs used should always be written/printed to help identify problem areas with specific sounds. For example, if the teacher presents *bag* and *tag*, the child should say "Yes." But if the teacher presents *bag* and *bun*, the child should respond "No."

To conduct informal individual assessments of student ability to identify word-initial phonemes, the teacher first gives an example, such as, "Some words start with the same sound, like *fun* and *fat* both start with /f/." The teacher then says, "I'm going to say two words. I want you to tell me if they start with the same sound. Let's try one: Do the words *boat* and box start with the same sound?" The teacher uses a simple checklist. Numbering each word pair presented, the teacher marks each of the student's answers correct/incorrect. It is important to write the actual words used, to facilitate identifying patterns of difficulty a student might have with certain sounds for remediation via direct instruction. This can also sometimes reveal undiagnosed hearing impairments or auditory processing disorders. The teacher presents correct pairs like *pig* and *pen,* and incorrect pairs like *hat* and *man.* Teachers can periodically repeat this assessment to monitor progress, and use the results to target specific problem phonemes for remediation.

For assessing blending, the teacher tells the student, "Let's play 'Guess My Word.' I'm going to say a word, but I'm going to say it in parts. I want you to guess what the word is. Here's an example: /c/--/at/." Can you guess the word?" The teacher uses a simple, numbered checklist. For each numbered item, the teacher has pre-written/printed the two sounds to present, such as /s/ and /un/, /b/ and /all/, etc. The teacher marks the student's response to each item as Correct or Incorrect. For phoneme segmentation, the teacher says, "I'm going to say a word. I want you to separate the word into the different sounds you hear. Let's practice: If I say 'cat,' you would say, /c/-/a/-/t/." The teacher presents a series of one-syllable words, which s/he has pre-written/printed on a checklist similar to the blending checklist, and marks the student's responses as correct/incorrect. Both assessments can be repeated periodically. Teachers can also analyze student responses for specific problem areas to remediate.

For phonemic manipulation skills, the teacher can tell the student that in the word game they will play, "I'll say a word. I want you to change the word's first sound to /s/. Let's practice first. If I said *cat,* then you would say *sat.*" The teacher has written a series of such simple, monosyllabic words on a numbered checklist, with the correct answer next to each, and lines/boxes/columns next to that to mark the student response as Correct or Incorrect.

- 68 -

For example, the correct response in this example for *run* would be *sun*. For phoneme deletion, the teacher tells the student, "I'll say a word. I want you to say it without the first sound. Let's practice: If I said *fun*, you would say *un*." The teacher then presents a series of similar short words pre-written/printed on a checklist like the one for phoneme manipulation, with the correct answers and places to mark student responses Correct/Incorrect. Teachers can re-use these assessments to monitor student progress.

Portfolio assessment

A portfolio assessment is not a test. Rather, it is a way for a teacher to collect a cumulative, concrete record of what a student can do. For example, the teacher might assign a student to make drawings, paintings, collages/other artworks related to a content-area topic or discipline. The teacher might assign the student to write essays on a given topic/content subject. Additionally, the student could construct three-dimensional objects related to a learning area. S/he could conduct a scientific experiment; the student and/or teacher take photos of its stages/steps; the student writes up his/her results and conclusions. All of these are examples of student products a teacher can include in the portfolio. This provides concrete results of the student's learning and skills progress over time—shorter intervals, a whole school year, even multiple years in some programs. Progress is more readily visual, concrete, and multi-dimensional than series of test scores. Portfolio assessments can benefit students lacking verbal skills, and students often derive pride from reviewing their products.

Constructed-response measurements

In constructed-response measures, the teacher might give students test questions and/or assign essays to write. However, these responses are not open-ended: the teacher provides directions guiding the student's construction of each response. This gives the students a structural framework within which to work. Constructed-response questions and/or directions are especially helpful for students who have difficulty organizing their thoughts; distinguishing main ideas from details; or selecting which information to include and which to omit. This method also gives students practice with such structural elements as creating a topic sentence, writing an introduction, paragraphing, writing transitions between paragraphs, and writing a conclusion sentence. It helps students stick to the subject if their thoughts and writing tend to wander. It also demonstrates the student's ability to follow instructions. In addition, reviewing a series of the same student's constructed responses over time can help the teacher and student monitor the student's progress by observing improvements in the organization, clarity, and detail of successive measures.

On demand writing

When teachers assign process writing, students focus on experiencing and practicing the steps of writing as a part of learning to write. They are not constrained by the time and content limits of on-demand writing tasks that are parts of standardized tests, such as the exit examinations required to earn high school graduation. On-demand writing tasks are also common components of college examinations and employer evaluations used to determine applicant hiring. Though on-demand writing is less natural and more pressured, creating anxiety and stress, it is necessary for teachers to give students practice in it to prepare them for its inevitable appearance on such high-stakes tests. For example, when students in seventh grade in some public schools are given exams, these may include such applications of writing as writing a summary; writing a narrative; writing a persuasive essay; and writing a response to literature essay. Teachers need to instruct students in both writing complete process papers, and practicing on-demand writing, for each of these applications.

In addition to giving students practice in the kinds of on-demand writing that will be expected of them on many standardized writing tests, teachers must also develop a common instructional language to use in writing direction words. To prepare students by familiarizing them with the kind of language they will encounter in such direct writing assessments, teachers should review the writing prompts used in these tests. Writing prompts are technically termed "on-demand release questions." Because the great majority of on-demand writing tasks used with fourth-graders through college students require writing informational and persuasive essays, teachers should focus on essay format in both the process papers and the on-demand writing they assign. They should particularly focus on teaching students how to write and practice writing thesis statements, which are the linchpins of effective essays. Teachers should instruct students in how to analyze writing prompts, use the language of the prompts, and form concise, specific thesis statements of the perspective or purpose of their essay.

Most on-demand writing assessments for students from elementary school through college demand the writing of persuasive and informational essays. Therefore, it is crucial for students to learn the structure of these essay genres. Teachers should provide students with a basic model of essay structure that is flexible enough for them to adapt to whichever essay form is required by the specific writing prompt in a test. For instance, the same structural foundation can be used for a persuasive essay or a response to literature essay, with some minor adjustments such as incorporating a counterpoint argument in the persuasive form, or inserting quotations and/or paraphrases in the response to literature form. There are even step-by-step guides available online and in print, which teachers may follow to help students learn how to memorize the structural parts and their sequence in essay writing. Teachers should have students practice every stage of the process of on-demand writing in isolation; in sequenced portions; and overall.

Teachers should give their students practice in the stages of the on-demand writing process, such as analyzing the writing prompts given; reading a passage when applicable; formulating the thesis statement for their essay; pre-writing the paragraphs of the essay's body; composing their essay; revising and proofreading. This practice helps develop student writing fluency and flexibility. Teachers should vary student practice to include both loosely timed exercises, interrupted by instructions; and strictly timed exercises without interruptions. Students also need practice in time management, which does not come naturally. Teachers can have students close their eyes and silently raise their hands when they think two minutes have elapsed, monitoring the times with the help of teacher aides or a few selected students. Student time-gauging will improve in accuracy if this exercise is practiced weekly. Assigning durations to each writing component, and having students practice in simulated testing conditions, will prepare students for real tests with experience and confidence.

For on-demand writing tasks in timed tests, students may either skip pre-writing because they gain no points from it; or pre-write excessively, robbing them of time for composition. To prevent such mishaps during formal testing, teachers can have students practice the parts and steps of writing essays in advance while simulating the conditions of the actual test. Allowing certain amounts of time for each part, and having students practice, will give them a better sense of how to manage their time under pressure. Teachers should also instruct students to write abundantly. Contrary to the usual advice to keep writing concise, direct writing assignments do not benefit from brevity. Standardized test graders are trained in carefully reading a student's thesis statement; skim the essay for arguments and/or main points; search for evidence supporting arguments and points; and read essay conclusions quickly. Teachers should advise their students to focus on their reader audience, use all of the time allowed them, and provide them with reinforcements (rewards) for doing this.

For on-demand direct writing, teachers should model specificity in writing and have students practice, using specific descriptions in narrative writing and providing a variety of evidence for argumentative/persuasive and informational essays. Students also need to learn how to create transitions—within sentences, at sentence beginnings and endings, between sentences, and between paragraphs—to unify their essays and make them coherent. Experts advise teachers to display prominently a poster in the classroom showing categories of transitions, and to refer often to these categories and to examples of transitions. Teachers should also have students practice in writing without transitions, and in revising writing that lacks specificity. Another expert tip is for teachers to instruct students in varying their sentence structures. Following the "50-50 Rule," 50% of sentences should be succinct, with a subject, verb, and complement. The other 50% should be expanded sentences, using a variety of grammatical sentence openers. Teachers should instruct students in grammatical sentence openers suitable to their grade levels that will be the most useful to them.

Stress management for direct writing assessments

Students usually realize that direct writing assessments constitute testing that is high-stakes, for themselves, for the school, or both. This knowledge normally generates test anxiety, which can limit students' success or even paralyze them. When giving students practice on on-demand writing tasks, teachers are advised to maintain a positive instructional focus. Teachers can help students change their attitudes toward the actual assessment. For instance, teachers can explain to students that anxiety and excitement share the same physiological responses, and encourage them to choose the idea that they are excited rather than anxious about the challenge of taking the test. Teachers should communicate their high standards to students, but at the same time communicate their belief in the students' competence to meet these high teacher expectations. Using the behavioral principle of successive approximations helps students develop self-confidence, as they experience success with each separate step and component of on-demand writing. Teachers should also communicate to students the validity of their own unique perspectives and voices they express in their essays.

Running record

Teachers can assess a student's current reading performance by taking running records as the student reads aloud. For purposes of conducting running record assessments, some books have been selected for use, called benchmark books. These are published with accompanying running record forms, with text excerpts from the books pre-printed on them. The first 100-150 words of a benchmark book are typically used for running records in higher grades. For teachers wanting to use more text, or different books, publishers also provide blank forms. The teacher annotates the form with marks showing correct and incorrect word reading; error types, such as omission, insertion, substitution, or repetition; self-corrections; saying a word's initial phoneme first; and interventions. Teachers also can note, if desired, the types of cues—meaning, structural, and visual—the student uses, to analyze student reading behavior and gain deeper understanding of reading problems, as applicable. Experts consider unfamiliar grade-level fiction and nonfiction books more accurate indices of student reading ability. Teachers may use familiar texts for some students if they prefer.

Experts recommend early emergent readers be assessed with running records of their reading every 2-4 weeks; emergent readers every 4-6 weeks; early fluent readers every 6-8 weeks; and fluent readers every 8-10 weeks. Teachers pick a book close to the student's reading level, telling the student to read aloud as the teacher observes and records notes. The teacher sits alongside the student to view text and student eye and finger movements. The teacher check-marks each correctly read word. If the student reads a word incorrectly, the teacher writes above that word what the student read. If a student reads too rapidly for teacher recording, the teacher asks him/her to pause until the teacher has caught up the recording. Teachers attend to reader behavior, like whether s/he is using visual, structural, and/or meaning cues for decoding and comprehension. Teachers make minimal interruptions/interventions. If the student gets stuck on a word, teachers wait 5-10 seconds and then, say the word. If the student is confused, explain and have him/her try again.

On the running record form, the teacher places a check-mark above every word read correctly. Word substitutions without self-correction count as one error regardless of number; the teacher writes the substitution(s) above the word. The teacher places a long dash above any word the student omits. If the student inserts an extra word, the teacher marks the location with a caret, writing the inserted word above it. Word repetitions are marked R; two repetitions are R2, three repetitions R3. Phrase repetitions are marked R with an arrow pointing to where the repetition began. Marking SC following an error denotes student self-correction. If the teacher must intervene, saying "Try again," s/he brackets the problematic text, marking TA above. If the teacher must intervene, telling the student a word after 5-10 seconds, s/he marks a T above the word. If the student says a word's initial sound first, the teacher marks that initial sound above the word, following with a check-mark if the student then says the word.

When a student considers the background of a story or other text s/he reads aloud; the information in text illustrations; and/or what particular sentences mean, s/he is using meaning cues. When the teacher observes this reading behavior, s/he marks M on the running record form. When the student uses his/her implicit knowledge of sentence structure and syntax to determine whether his/her reading sounds right, this is using structural cues; teachers mark S. Observing word-initial letters/sounds, letters' and words' appearances, word lengths, familiar phrases, etc., constitutes using visual cues; teachers mark V. The teacher's first step is checking correctly read words and marking errors on the form. Teachers should first familiarize themselves with the symbols and marking conventions used. It also helps to practice with another teacher who plays the role of the student reading aloud and purposely makes errors to record. The second step, based on the first step's markings, is filling the form's boxes for each sentence/line read: number of errors, self-corrections, and M/S/V cues used for each error/self-correction.

After recording correctly read words, errors and error types, etc., the teacher totals the student's number of errors and self-corrections. To calculate the student's error rate, divide the total number of words read by the total number of errors made. The ratio errors: words expresses how many words were read correctly per error; for example, 100 words read/10 errors = 1:10, meaning that for each error, the student read 10 words correctly. The formula for accuracy rate, expressed as a percentage, is total words read minus total errors, divided by total words read; for instance, (100 words – 10 errors)/100 = 90/100 = .90 = 90% accuracy. This rate can be compared against text difficulty: Independent-level reading = 95-100% accuracy rate; Instructional-level = 90-94%; and Frustration-level = 89% or lower. Self-correction rate, expressed as a ratio, is calculated with the formula (Number of errors + number of self-corrections)/number of self-corrections; for example, (10 + 5)/5 = 15/5 = 3; self-correction rate = 1:3, or 1 self-correction for every 3 errors. Self-correction rates of 1:4 or lower show that students are self-monitoring their reading.

In addition to quantitatively calculating a student's accuracy rate, error rate, and self-correction rate, a teacher can also make a qualitative analysis of the student's reading development through taking a running record of the student reading aloud. While taking the running record, the teacher has observed the student's reading behaviors and marked whenever s/he observed the student using visual (V), structural (S), and/or meaning (M) cues to help decode and comprehend what s/he read aloud. In addition to how the student used these cues, the teacher has also paid attention to the student's reading fluency, phrasing, and intonational patterns while reading aloud. Moreover, using the notations s/he made and his/her memory of the reading, the teacher considers what kinds of prompts s/he gave to help the student when needed and how the student responded to each prompt and prompt type. Combining all these observations informs the teacher's qualitative analysis of the student's reading to formulate an overall picture of student reading development.

Miscue analysis

K. S. Goodman (1969) developed and named the approach of miscue analysis, which is used to examine a reader's specific strategies. Wrong guesses, i.e. miscues, made by a student when reading a text aloud, contain information that can inform the listener/teacher as to how hard/easy the student finds the text to read; and how unfamiliar/familiar the student is with the text's content. This information gained from analyzing miscues is not available from standard reading test results, because reading entails far more than simply examining every letter and word closely. Goodman identified three cueing systems as foundations of the reading process: (1) letter-to-sound relationships, i.e. the **grapho/phonic** cueing system; (2) sentence structure, word order, and grammar—i.e. the **syntactic** cueing system; and (3) the meanings we recognize from words, i.e. the **semantic** cueing system. Goodman proposed that patterns in a reader's miscues/mistakes reveal both weaknesses and strengths; and that through these miscues, combined with what s/he can describe about how s/he made them, we can understand the learner's reading process.

Miscue analysis (Goodman, 1969) focuses on the types of errors readers make for information about the learner's reading skills and strategies. For example, substituting "the machine's performance" for text "the machine's programming"; "reading for instructions" for "ready for instructions"; "hadn't changed" for "hated changes"; "clean" for "clear", but then corrects this; and immediately self-corrects "found" to "fond", has substituted noun for noun, adjective for adjective, and verb form for verb form. S/he has substituted words resembling the correct ones, not drastically changing the meaning. The reader also self-

- 73 -

corrected as soon as s/he found that certain errors made no sense in context. This reader reads for meaning by using all three cueing systems—grapho/phonic, or how words look; semantic, or what words mean; and syntactic, or how words sound and are organized. Conversely, a reader who substitutes "dropped on" with "dropping from"; "planes" with "plans"; "horses" with "arches"; "really" with "already"; "more" with "move"; "to" with "the"; and "cinema" with "camera" substitutes mostly similar-looking words, disregarding the meaning.

Using miscue analysis can show differential reading proficiency in different students, but not from counting each student's miscues/errors. For example, two students might make the same number of reading errors; but by analyzing their miscues, we discover one seeks meaning while reading, whereas the other seeks simply to complete the reading whether it makes sense or not. One reader substitutes incorrect words very similar in appearance, sound, and meaning to the correct ones, and/or self-corrects misread words when they make no sense in context. This student reads for meaning. The other reader substitutes incorrect words that look similar to the correct ones, but are grammatically wrong and/or have no meaning in their context. Such a reader may also decode as s/he reads, or read word-for-word. This student does not read for meaning. One strategy is using a cloze procedure, i.e. short passages with gaps to fill. This helps the student focusing mainly on letter/word appearances to predict also the contextual, semantic cues and syntactic, grammatical cues that facilitate finding meaning.

Experts caution that beginning readers are not good candidates for the use of miscue analysis as a reading assessment. Early readers may not have developed an understanding of phonics sufficient for decoding printed language and must depend completely on semantic (meaning) cues in text. Additionally, researchers find students with inadequate reading skills rely less on contextual cues for reading comprehension and fluency; so miscue analysis would yield little useful information about their reading either. When miscue analysis is appropriate, experts recommend giving students a choice of 3-4 texts. Fewer can prevent students from selecting text they prefer; more can be overwhelming. In general, guidelines are to give students at lower (applicable) entry reading levels passages of around 100 words or so; around 200 words at upper entry levels; and longer selections at higher reading levels. Assessing educators should secure about 30 minutes in a quiet room without interruptions (including ringing phones); good lighting; a recorder with good sound quality; and clear copies of text for reading and scoring.

The three cueing systems identified by Goodman (1969) in his method of miscue analysis are grapho/phonic, semantic, and syntactic. In the grapho/phonic cueing system, the appearances of words are their salient features. A student who makes miscues (errors) that have effective grapho/phonic similarities might substitute the word "owning" for the text word "owing"; "strengthened" for "straightened"; "determent" for "detriment"; and/or "wrist" for "waist". Here the miscued words are very similar in shape, length, and meaning to the text words. Miscues with partial grapho/phonic similarities include mistaking "fortitude" for "fortunate"; "present" for "patient"; "acclimatization" for "accumulation"; and/or "sedately" for "sadly". These differ more in appearance and meaning than those with effective similarities (above). Miscues having little or no grapho/phonic similarity include mistaking "usual" for "surface"; "present" for "perched"; "flickering" for "blinking"; and/or "almost" for "awfully". The less similarity between the text's original word and the reader's miscue, the more likely the text author's intention will be lost or misconstrued, and the less likely the reader will comprehend the text's meaning.

Miscue analysis focuses on the three cueing systems identified by its author Goodman (1969): grapho/phonic, semantic, and syntactic. In the semantic system, meaning is the key factor. When reading aloud, the errors/miscues a student makes can vary in how semantically strong they are, i.e. how much they affect the text's meaning. When a student's miscues do not alter the text author's meaning significantly, they are viewed as having high semantic strength and acceptability. For example, the student might read "destructive" instead of "disruptive," volcanic" instead of "violent," or "offer" instead of "afford". Miscues with partial semantic acceptability or strength seem suitable within one phrase, clause, or sentence but not the text's overall context. These include, for example, reading "horse" for "house"; "penguins" for "pigeons"; "special" for "species"; or "regarded" for "rewarded". Miscues with poor semantic strength include reading "pigments" for "pigeons"; "parent" for "present"; or "over" for "owner". These are less acceptable because the miscues share less meaning with the original words in the text.

To assess reading problems, miscue analysis (Goodman, 1969) divides reading into three coding or cueing systems: grapho/phonic, semantic, and syntactic. The syntactic cueing system supplies information about whether words/phrases/clauses function grammatically within the context of their sentences. A student may misread some words orally, yet demonstrate the recognition that the incorrect words fit the sentence's syntax as well as the text's original words. For example, syntactically strong miscues include these: misreading text that says "He had huge arms" as "He had huge hands"; misreading "It was fully mature" as "It was finally mature"; or misreading "...to send her as a present" as "...to send her as a patient". These incorrect words still fit the sentences' grammatical contexts. Syntactically weak miscues, by contrast, include reading "...both sides of his face" as "...besides of his face"; "He was completely devoid of hair" as "He was completely devote of hair"; or "...a glitter of ironic laughter" as "...a greater of ironic laughter". These substitutions are grammatically as well as semantically incorrect.

In addition to recording which words were omitted; which substituted and with what; which words were inserted; and words where the reader does not respond, the teacher should also observe the following reader behaviors in the student: Whether or not the student reads one word at a time; if the student reads aloud in a jerky manner; if the student uses inappropriate or absent intonational variations; whether the student misses lines while reading and/or loses his/her place in the text; whether the student observes punctuation in the text when reading aloud, or fails to pause and to change pitch, etc., accordingly with punctuation marks; whether the student places vocal stress on each and every syllable; whether the student reads fluently, hesitating only before challenging words, or reads hesitantly overall; whether or not the student pauses after phrases/clauses and sentences; and most of all, whether the student comprehends the meaning of the overall text or not. The teacher should record Yes/No to these based on observations of the student reading aloud.

Miscue analysis classifies reading errors into different categories, e.g., insertion, substitution, omission, repetition, reversal, hesitation, and self-correction. One such category is non-response. According to miscue analysis (Goodman, 1969), a student who fails to respond lacks understanding of the grapho/phonic (letter-to-sound) system, limiting his/her word-attack skills. The student uses sight words, limiting his/her attack to the visual modality without accompanying sound/phonic information. Students who fail to respond upon encountering unknown words are afraid to guess, so they likely also do not avail themselves of contextual cues. They are also characterized as anxious readers who do not want to experience public "failure." The teacher should ask the student whether s/he attempts to decipher unknown words by: analyzing letter-to-sound relationships; identifying letter clusters and syllables within a word; identifying smaller words contained within larger words; using visual analogies (e.g., "hard" looks like "card"); using the syntax to predict likely word choices; and/or using the content to predict likely words. This questioning reveals what processes occur in the student upon encountering unknown words.

According to miscue analysis of reading (Goodman, 1969), if a student misreads some words, but the words s/he substitutes have similar appearances, sounds, *and* meanings to the original text words, this may suggest that the student is attacking the text impulsively and/or hurriedly. The solution is to encourage the student to slow down a little when reading. However, if the student makes errors by substituting words very different from the original text, s/he is likely to have poor skills in the grapho/phonic cueing system—i.e. poor knowledge or understanding of letter-to-sound relationships—and in addition is not compensating for these by using the surrounding sentence and passage context to predict what word(s) are likely in that context. Direct instruction in grapho-phonemic relationships, and in attending to context, are indicated. If a student's miscues involve familiar, common, and small words, this can show that the student's sight vocabulary is weak and needs further development through intensive instruction and practice.

According to Goodman's (1969) miscue analysis, one reason some students insert extraneous words into the text they read aloud is that they are attracted to the future word(s) in a sentence and are prematurely trying to incorporate it to their sense of semantic acceptability—that is, have it make sense in context in terms of meaning. Another factor to consider is that readers fluent enough not to read one word at a time might be reading a bit too quickly, leading to insertion miscues. The author cautions the teacher not to over-emphasize such student insertion errors if they do not significantly alter the meaning of the text. However, at the same time, the teacher must consider whether the student's insertion miscues are syntactic in nature (for example, morphological insertions like changing the word "full" to the word "fully"), because such structural additions can change the sentence meaning. When this is the case, the teacher needs to point out to the student the differences in meaning produced by the insertion.

According to the miscue analysis model (Goodman, 1969), miscues/errors involving word omission can be made by a student who reads a little bit faster than his or her proficiency allows for accuracy. Omissions can also occur when the reader has a weak sight word vocabulary. When leaving out small and regular words does not change the meaning of the text, teachers can overlook these student oversights. However, it is important for teachers to remember how the meaning of a sentence, clause, or phrase can be changed—indeed, completely reversed—when the reader omits such a word as "not". Teachers should observe whether the student consistently or frequently omits entire lines rather than just single words: omission of whole lines can indicate poor skills with eye tracking. This can sometimes also indicate additional problems, such as visual field defects interrupt and/or truncate eye tracking. For further analysis, teachers should also observe where students omit words: before unfamiliar/challenging words; in the middle of passages; and/or at the ends of lines.

According to miscue analysis, good readers search for meaning in text and seek to consolidate meaning; therefore, some repetitions indicate good reading skills/strategies. However, if a student repeats too often, the text may be too difficult, sacrificing fluency to attain comprehension. In addition to adjusting text difficulty levels, teachers should observe whether a student repeats just before a harder word; this can indicate the student is stalling for time in order to decode it. Similarly to repetitions, corrections also demonstrate awareness of the text's meaning in good readers. However, overly frequent self-corrections can mean the student is reading a bit too rapidly. They can also mean the reader is responding to the visual shapes of words prematurely to considering their meanings. Excessive self-corrections can compromise the student's reading comprehension, even when corrections do not change the text meaning. Another consideration is that students who do not perceive themselves as good readers may correct their reading even when it was already accurate.

According to miscue analysis, students may reverse words or phrases in a sentence without affecting the text's overall meaning, in which case the author (Goodman, 1969) finds little cause for concern. However, the author also points out that some word and phrase reversals will change the syntax or grammar of the sentence. The student's response to this altered word order and sentence structure can often be to try to make up for the change in the sentence's sequence of ideas by forcing alternative verb endings and other such morphological changes. At times when a student reverses letters within a single word, such as reading "saw" for "was", this will not substantially affect the meaning of the sentence; however, at other times it will do so, such as reading "no" instead of "on". Research finds that students are likely to make such reversals more frequently with short words that are used most often (i.e., "high-frequency" words) in printed text.

According to Goodman (1969)'s miscue analysis model, students who do not perceive themselves as good reader tend to hesitate when reading aloud due to lack of self-confidence. Students with weak visual skills are more likely to hesitate. Students with deficient grapho/phonic skills, i.e. understanding and applying the relationships of written letters to spoken sounds, are also more likely to hesitate during reading aloud. Another factor contributing to reading hesitation is text difficulty. While in some cases the teacher can provide less challenging text, in many cases—especially in secondary school grades—content-area courses require the reading of specified texts, making it inevitable that some students read some texts too difficult for their individual reading skills. Teachers can glean further information about the student's reading behavior by observing where s/he hesitates in reading. Always hesitating before unknown/challenging words indicates the student knows and is preparing for what is coming. Always hesitating at the beginnings/ends of lines may reveal the student has difficulties with smoothly eye-tracking the text.

Miscue analysis finds student Alex attempts every word in the text; comprehends the text's main meanings; recognizes punctuation; and makes some self-corrections. That many of Alex's substitution errors use visually similar words—of similar length and shape, with the same initial letters—indicate his primary word-recognition strategies are visual. Alex also sometimes uses semantic cues, i.e. meaning in the text, to decipher words, evidenced by substituting words he knows for similar, unfamiliar ones. However, he sometimes also misreads words/phrases with substitutions making no sense. Alex's knowledge of letter-to-sound relationships is shaky; for this reason, he does not effectively apply decoding strategies to new words. He reads words holistically without closely analyzing their components and, for this reason, he omits suffixes, plural endings, etc. This changes the

- 77 -

grammar, so he must then change subsequent words to fit. Instruction in advance text scanning, analyzing word features and meanings, and discussing possible text content can increase his reading comprehension and fluency.

IEP goals

Student Alex's strengths include text punctuation awareness; attempting every word; comprehending the gist of text; some self-correction; and sometimes using semantic cues to decode words. Weaknesses include inadequate grapho/phonic (letter-to-sound) understanding, inhibiting decoding unfamiliar words; reading words holistically, disregarding morphological differences that change meaning; and disregarding the lack of meaning in some of his errors. Alex's primary decoding strategies are visual. He needs help working on detailed analysis of word parts and meanings, scanning text in advance, and predicting text content. An example of a long-term IEP goal for Alex is: to read familiar and meaningful texts at ___ Level (insert the student's target reading level) with little hesitation and with comprehension. Examples of short-term IEP goals include: to identify main ideas and points, and predict words from context; to scan texts to find key and/or challenging words; to apply varied strategies to decode increasingly larger ranges of new words, especially emphasizing syllables, suffixes, and letter and sound patterns; and to look up new words in the dictionary.

Student self-evaluations

When students at any reading level have no idea yet how to use fundamental reading strategies, such as phonemic awareness or the alphabetic principle, to decode printed language, they are likely not ready for self-evaluation, let alone applying it to remedial efforts. However, once any student has gained some experience with attempting to read aloud and receiving evaluations and corrections from a teacher, the teacher can introduce the student to principles and practices of self-evaluation, and the self-correction it informs. Very young beginning readers are in earlier stages of cognitive development and often cannot view/analyze their reading processes objectively. However, teachers can instruct them in simpler, more concrete self-evaluations, such as identifying their errors as they read aloud. Teachers begin by correcting younger students, and then gradually introducing questions and directions guiding them to identify all individual letters in a word; sound out the word; decide whether their reading of a word makes sense in the context, etc. Students will eventually internalize these practices as self-monitoring habits, improving their literacy skills.

Anecdotal records

Anecdotal records cannot replace formal/informal reading tests/inventories or other assessment instruments, but can provide valuable supplements to these. For example, whenever a teacher, teacher's aide, specialist, therapist, or other personnel who interact with students during reading-related activities notices a specific student reading behavior, or a recurring pattern in the student's reading behaviors, s/he can record it by simply writing down an account of what s/he observed. Personnel other than the student's teacher should share this information with the teacher, who can also include it in the student's records after reviewing and considering it. Anecdotal records differ from other assessment instruments in that they do not involve quantitative measurements, such as computing all numbers of errors, error types, etc. Anecdotal records do not require statistical proof of validity or reliability, or compare student performance to a norm or a criterion. An anecdote is simply a narrative description of an event or incident. Educators can often glean important clues about student reading problems/behaviors from analyzing anecdotal reports after they are made.

Keeping a journal

By keeping a journal, a student can record such things as: the particular errors and/or kinds of errors s/he is making on any given day; the particular mistakes s/he corrected successfully that day; the specific successes s/he experienced with reading; how many new vocabulary words s/he has learned; the feelings, such as frustration, anger, sadness, inadequacy, s/he experiences when struggling with reading; and the feelings of control, happiness, excitement, mastery, and higher self-esteem and self-efficacy s/he experiences accompanying improvements in reading. Journal writing enables a student to reflect on his/her progress, both on a daily basis and over time. Similarly to the way a student can gain both insights and pride by reviewing his/her cumulative work products in a portfolio assessment, the student can reread his/her journal entries over a time period of time and realize his/her improvements.   Journaling allows a student to increase self-corrections, and also to reflect on his/her reading behaviors—developing metacognition, i.e., thinking about thinking and understanding the nature of one's own thought and learning processes.

Validity and reliability with respect to assessment

Validity and reliability are properties required in designing experimental studies and assessment instruments. Validity means that an instrument actually measures what it is intended to measure. For example, rulers for measuring length and scales for measuring weight are valid instruments. This specific kind of validity is called measurement validity. Reliability, on the other hand, means that an instrument is consistent across administrations. For example, if you give a class of students a certain test, and then give the same class the same test at a later date under similar conditions, the results of both administrations should be similar. If you measure the same concrete object with the same ruler over time, you will get the same measurement every time. But a student can take a standardized test, like the SAT or GRE, at different times and get very different scores, influenced by various factors. Thus such standardized tests have less measurement reliability than rulers do. An instrument can be valid but not reliable, or reliable but not valid.

Validity is how much a test measures what it purports to measure. Content validity refers to whether/how much a test's items are representative of the full range of possible test items. A test whose items only cover a small portion of the skill set or topic does not have strong content validity. Construct validity is how well a test's scores predict a theoretical construct, such as intelligence, for example: any intelligence test should have strong construct validity. Criterion validity refers to how effectively a test measures some variable/quality according to a given criterion. Criterion validity includes concurrent and predictive validity. When test scores and criterion measurements are made at the same time (concurrently), these indicate the extent of concurrent validity. For example, a test to measure an individual's anxiety levels has concurrent validity if its scores match the current anxiety levels the test-taker is experiencing. Predictive validity involves measuring criteria after test administration. For example, scholastic/career aptitude tests can predict later failure/success in specific academic subjects/occupations.

Reliability is the extent to which a research study or a test instrument is consistent or repeatable, meaning the extent to which it yields accurate measurements across a range. Four types of reliability are: (1) inter-rater reliability, meaning that if the same test is given to different people, the results will be consistent across test-takers; (2) test-retest reliability, meaning that if the same people are given the same test at different times, their scores will be consistent across administrations; (3) parallel-forms reliability, meaning that different individuals are given different tests at the same time to measure the same things, and the results are consistent across test-takers and test forms; (4) internal consistency reliability, meaning that the test-takers are evaluated using different test questions, but all questions are based on the same construct, concept, or idea. This compares individual questions to each other for their capacity to obtain consistent and appropriate results.

Internal and external validity

Validity is whether an instrument measures what it is meant to measure. Internal validity is whether one can infer causal relationships between an intervention and results obtained. For example, researchers test baseline reading levels in a group of students; introduce an instructional intervention; and re-test these students with the same testing instrument. They must be able to determine whether any increases/decreases in student scores are directly attributable to the intervention or not. To eliminate selection bias as a factor, researchers randomly select the participants; each student has an equal chance of being selected or not. Researchers also designate a treatment group to receive the intervention, and a control group receiving no intervention. With random selection, researchers know any differences between these two groups are only through chance, not bias. External validity is whether a study's results are generalizable to the general population. For example, an intervention's effects on rural Alabama students are unlikely to apply to private-school students in Los Angeles or public-school students in New York City.

Inter-rater reliability

Inter-rater reliability assesses the amount of reliability there exists across different individual people. It applies when multiple persons are taking or giving a test or a measurement. For example, when an experimental study uses individual people to observe and record the outcomes or behaviors of the other study participants who are being tested, and/or receiving some kind of intervention which the researchers are evaluating for effectiveness—in which case participants take the same test before and after receiving the intervention, and their scores are compared to those of a control group not receiving that intervention—inter-rater reliability is important. Two primary ways of using inter-rater reliability are testing similarity in how individuals categorize things; and testing similarity in how individuals score test items. An advantage of inter-rater reliability is detecting observer biases, which easily interfere when observation is a designated method. A disadvantage is that it only applies to multiple observers/raters, whereas some studies/tests involve single observers/raters.

Test-retest reliability

Test-retest reliability is how consistent a test is across time. Variables that affect a test-taker's scores on repeated administrations of the same test at different times include the time of day when the test is given; whether the test-taker has slept well before testing;

whether and what the test-taker has eaten before testing; whether there are interruptions during administration, how many and what kind; testing conditions like room temperature, lighting; noise/other distractions; the test-taker's mood, etc. Tests very sensitive to such variables yield widely different ranges of results—even if administrations are only ½ hour apart—showing poor test-retest reliability. More reliable tests yield comparatively little variance despite such factors. A disadvantage is that over enough time, test-takers mature cognitively and learn more, producing different retest results. This method is often used for pre-test and post-test measures in experiments using non-treated control groups. Researchers evaluate different individual personality-test items, or various national scholastic tests of the same abilities, by administering them to the same students over several years.

Parallel-forms reliability

When educational experts are developing assessment instruments, one problem they often encounter is determining which questions or items are the best ones to assess the test-taker's knowledge or abilities. One way that they can find this out is to use parallel forms, i.e., designing two different tests that use different questions, items, or sets of questions/items that assess the same concept or construct. For example, an educational researcher might come up with a large number of questions or items on a subject or ability. Then, the researcher divides this large set of items/questions in half; and administers each one to one half of a sample of individuals s/he has targeted for assessing on the designated measures, and has assigned randomly. When researchers are developing national standardized tests, they commonly administer two different tests at the same time to their selected participants. Whichever test yields the most consistent results across test-takers is chosen. If the other test has adequate consistency, they use it as a backup instrument.

Research questions

The purpose of asking research questions is to evaluate their answers according to an established idea/concept/construct. When various research questions are posed, if they all test the same construct despite being different, then they all should yield consistent results. When individual test questions/items are compared and their results are appropriate and consistent with one another, these items have good internal consistency reliability. (1) Average inter-item correlation pairs questions measuring the same construct; obtains correlations between the members of each pair; and computes the mean/average of all pairs' correlations for comparison. (2) Average item total correlation computes a total score for each item in the average inter-item correlations (above), and averages these total scores. (3) Split-half correlation separates items testing the same construct into two tests, given to the same participants; then computes the correlation between the two groups' total scores. (4) Cronbach's alpha correlation computes an equivalent of the average of all possible split-half correlations (above), using the average of all Pearson product-moment correlation coefficients (r).

Communicating reading assessment results

The quality and amount of parental involvement at home with their children's education are influenced by teacher and school communication of reading assessment results. For example, when a teacher or school communicates more results and/or observations focusing on needs or weaknesses than those focusing on strengths or accomplishments, parents feel they cannot help their children and are discouraged from involving themselves. Teachers and schools also benefit parents by giving them ideas of how to support and assist their children, and informing parents more about school academic programs and how they function. Additionally, parents appreciate more the significance of their role in their children's education, and gain confidence regarding how valuable their involvement is, when teachers/schools communicate. Student benefits include greater motivation to learn, better attendance and behavior, and more positive attitudes overall about school. Teachers benefit when parent involvement frees them to focus on teaching more, informs them better about children's needs, and raises teacher morale through higher parental regard of teachers.

The increasing diversity of families in our society dictates that teachers cannot depend on only one communication method, but must have a variety of strategies to address varying family needs and schedules. Some of these include: sending periodic newsletters to parents/families; holding class/school open houses annually; hosting curriculum nights; making home visits when appropriate; making telephone calls—not just to discuss problems, but also to communicate positive results; creating annual school calendars for families; inserting messages to families in local newspapers; holding annual Grandparents Days and days for other significant persons; having a communications officer or spokesperson from the local Board of Education attend the school's PTA meetings; establishing "homework hotlines" for students to contact by telephone and/or online; having annual school field days; distributing handouts, bulletins and notices in local gathering places such as churches/temples/mosques, healthcare clinics, and food markets; setting up a website for the school; conducting workshops for parents; and directing communications not only to mothers, but fathers as well.

Teachers should inform students exactly what has been assessed, how, and when. They should communicate to students from the outset how grades will be determined, and the assessment procedures involved. Teachers should communicate to students their learning goals, and that enhancing their progress toward these goals is the purpose of assessment. For truly student-centered approaches, teachers must involve students in the assessment process, which includes inviting them to provide meaningful input regarding classroom assessment and grading. For example, students can indicate how they will show their competencies regarding course learning goals. Teachers can give students guidance in developing self-evaluation skills. Teachers can create and communicate assessment/grading criteria; collaborate with students to establish criteria; or students may negotiate or make their own criteria. Students typically gain motivation, insight, and achievement success through being involved. Teachers can share assessment information via both oral and written communications. Teachers should relate assessments to learning goals and subject content: students should know how assessment is integral to learning, and not experience assessments as surprises.

With large class sizes to manage and the myriad duties of fulfilling the general education curriculum, the classroom teacher might not have as much specific, detailed information about an individual student's reading characteristics. The classroom teacher may only have had time and responsibility to administer whole-class standardized reading tests, while the specialist could have obtained more individualized information from performing individual miscue analyses, running records, and other measures. Also, because students who struggle with reading especially need as much help as they can get, the specialist and generalist teachers can collaborate on instructional planning to improve literacy skills, providing more consistency between settings and activities as well as more time spent on reading-related work. Informing guidance counselors can help them counsel students about career aptitudes and preferences; whether students' subject grades accurately reflect their aptitude/ability scores; and feelings of failure/success. Speech-language pathologists can use detailed reading data to coordinate with assessing/remediating student hearing/production of specific speech sounds; auditory processing functions; reading-aloud fluency; intonation; breath control; voice production and quality, etc.

Communicating with students' families and other involved parties

Teachers should remember to communicate not only negative-sounding factors like needs/deficits to families, but positive attributes equally. Moreover, in initial conferences, teachers can better establish rapport and trust by beginning with positive statements about the student. It is helpful to frame needs as opportunities for further growth rather than evidence of "something wrong" with the student. While reading grade levels may be shared, rather than first presenting these on paper, it is better for teachers to explain orally to families what these do and do not imply: seeing only numbers, which may be far below age/grade level, they can misinterpret these as signs of mental retardation/other disorders in students who are intellectually average/above-average but may have learning disabilities, lack of literacy exposure, etc. When sharing data with families, teachers should feel expected not only to communicate their instructional plan, but also recruit families to collaborate in the student's education by reading together at home and playing literacy-related games; and provide families with resources for obtaining books and other literacy materials.

(1) Initiation: As soon as teachers know who their students will be each school year, they should initiate family contact. They can introduce themselves via letters, e-mails, or telephone calls. (2) Timeliness: Teachers, parents, and other involved adults should contact one another as soon as possible after observing a problem. Delays can exacerbate the problem and cause additional problems, including frustration. (3) Frequency and consistency: Parents, caregivers and other concerned parties want to be informed frequently, regularly, and on a continuing basis about students' homework and other performance measures. (4) Follow-through: Related to effective two-way communication, both parents/caregivers and teachers want the other to follow through on what they say they are going to do relative to student progress. Reciprocal trust both influences and is influenced by good reciprocal communication. (5) Clear and useful communication: Both families and teachers should receive the information that they require to assist and support the students, in formats and languages that they can understand and apply.

Reading Leadership

No Child Left Behind Act

Scientifically-based progress monitoring allows teachers to evaluate their own instruction's effectiveness, for whole classes or individual students. After identifying student goals for learning over time, teachers compare student progress against goals—i.e. expected vs. actual learning rates—and adjust their instruction accordingly. Progress monitoring affords benefits of more student-tailored teaching; higher teacher expectations of students; more informed teaching decisions; and, consequently, faster student learning. Teachers' student goals and their teaching techniques become more accurately targeted and efficient through progress monitoring, facilitating students' meeting state achievement standards more quickly. Moreover, NCLB's Adequate Yearly Progress (AYP) provision requires schools to demonstrate enough progress toward NCLB's goal of universal proficiency in reading (and math) by 2013-2014 for all public school students in third through eighth grades. Progress monitoring can be applied to evaluate the progress of a student/class/school toward meeting this AYP requirement. As the minimum yearly growth rate necessary to remove the difference between universal proficiency and a school's existing proficiency, AYP varies among schools; progress monitoring can help determine a school's AYP.

Since NCLB was enacted, educators have pursued increased interest in measuring and improving student learning through standards-based assessments. At first, educators concentrated on yearly, state-level standardized test results. However, they soon discovered that these findings were "too little, too late" for identifying students lagging behind grade/peer levels. But they discovered concurrently that classroom-level formative assessments could achieve statistically significant student learning progress. Experts identify benchmark assessment as the middle ground between state-level and classroom-level formative assessment. Benchmarks assessments are made at certain times during a curriculum sequence, throughout school years. They assess student skills and knowledge related to a specified group of long-term learning goals. The expected users of benchmark assessments, the purposes for their uses, and how the assessment instruments are used dictate the selection and design of benchmark assessments. These benchmark assessments can inform instructional planning, decisions at classroom/school/district levels, and educational policy.

Curriculum-Based Measurement

CBM furnishes methods to assess academic proficiency in reading, as well as in writing, spelling, and math. Whereas traditional assessments measure skills mastery, CBM focuses on fluency, and reflects changes in both response ease and accuracy in its scoring. Also, each score in CBM reflects *overall* proficiency in each academic subject. For example, CBM uses fluency in reading passages as a measure of overall reading proficiency because passage reading demands coordinating multi-dimensional reading skills like word recognition, decoding, and comprehension. CBM also affords modeling of academic improvement within a school year: Educators plot individual scores of regular weekly/monthly/quarterly CBM administrations on graphs, representing student progress rates as slopes. They connect a year-end goal, representing NCLB's AYP requirement, to a student's beginning CBM score, to create a goal line showing the desired improvement rate. When student scores drop below the goal line, teachers find their existing teaching programs insufficient, and adjust them toward increasing student learning rates.

Applying CBM to AYP requirement

NCLB mandates not only that all third- through eighth-grade public school students achieve "universal proficiency" in reading and math by 2013-2014, but moreover that schools make sufficient annual progress (AYP) toward universal proficiency. Educators can apply CBM to their efforts to meet the requirements of AYP in reading mandated by NCLB. They can also use CBM to monitor student progress toward meeting this AYP; and to integrate the accountability systems in general education and special education programs. Three steps recommended by experts for using CBM to meet AYP requirements are: (1) quantify initial school reading proficiency status by assessing each student with CBM, and identifying how many students initially attain CBM benchmarks. This constitutes the school's initial proficiency; (2) subtract this number from the total number of students to calculate the discrepancy between universal proficiency and initial school proficiency status; and (3) divide this discrepancy figure by the number of years until 2013-2014—the quotient equals how many more students must meet CBM end-of-year benchmarks every year, or AYP.

Accessing literacy research

Today, educators, students, and parents can avail themselves of a wealth of resources to access research into literacy development, especially online. For example, the website and company Education Planet offers a database containing over 100,000 instructional resources, e-learning services, and web tools approved by teachers. Teachers can use this site to share instructional ideas and experiences, learn additional ways to integrate technology into their curricula, and search more than 16,000 lesson plans. Education World's search engine can be filtered to search only educational websites. Education World also includes information on best classroom technology applications, lesson plans, educational experts' articles, education-related news items, website reviews, and job listings. Educators can search one million-plus records of educational theory, research, and practice in the ERIC Database via the Educator's Reference Desk website, as well as over 2,000 lesson plans, archives of 200+ question answers, and 3,000+ links to education information online. A website established by educators for disseminating educational information and resources, and offering free services to educators and students, is GreatTeacher.net.

Supporting school-wide reading initiatives

To achieve leadership in school-wide initiatives focused on the reading curriculum, educators should first be knowledgeable in the criteria for choosing a robust core reading program. They should ensure that whatever reading program they pick is effective enough to help the majority of students achieve success. They should also be able to identify how their school reading program demonstrates the "five big ideas" of reading (phonemic awareness, the alphabetic principle, fluency with text, vocabulary, and comprehension). School leaders should help the school's staff to select intervention and supplemental programs that have been proven effective by research-based evidence. Leaders should also support the school staff in developing and applying CSI maps. CSI stands for Core, Supplemental, and Intervention programs. CSI maps are grade-level plans indicating which

Core, Supplemental, and Intervention programs will be used in instruction; and for how many minutes per day these will be taught according to student instructional levels. Furthermore, school administrators and other non-teaching leaders should learn their curriculum as well as the teachers.

School administrators and other members of leadership should endeavor to learn as much as they can about the formative assessment(s) their school uses. Formative assessments reflect ongoing learning rather than what has been learned by end-of-lesson/unit/semester/year, which is measured by summative assessments. School leaders should learn how to gather data within their school's formative assessment system, and use this knowledge to help educators by periodically collecting data themselves. Members of leadership should also learn how to read and interpret the information in their data reports, and how to apply it to direct their school's instruction. They should also use the information in data reports for guiding regular planning meetings for each grade level in their school. To provide leadership in the area of reading assessment, they should also regularly engage in conversations with teachers about data collected regarding their students' performance in reading, discussing ideas with them for fine-tuning their instruction to make it most effective.

School administrators and others in leadership positions should regularly walk through their school's classrooms to get an idea of each teacher's reading instruction, focusing on its strengths and needs. Leaders should discuss teaching and learning, particularly that which is most reading-related, with their teachers. They should make it a point to provide teachers with plenty of praise, affirmation, and encouragement with regard to their reading instruction. Where they identify needs in teachers' instructional practices with reading, leaders should supply the additional training that the teachers require. According to experts, school administrators should support the practice of grouping students during reading lessons. Through judicious oversight and management of the school schedule, leaders should ensure enough time for reading instruction, and work towards preventing reading lessons from being interrupted. Leaders should support student outcomes more than their processes: as experts observe, "the process is only as good as the outcomes" (Paine, WETA 2012).

School leaders can increase students' motivation to read by visiting classrooms and reading to students, showing their and the school's commitment to reading, demonstrating its importance and enjoyment. They should visit classes during reading group activities, praising student successes. They can let students come to their offices to read. Leaders should read some of the same books their students are reading, and discuss the books with them. This not only shows students the leaders' interest in them and their interests; it also helps leaders learn about students' interests, opinions, and reading motivations. Leaders can use programs, such as Battle of the Books or Reading Counts, to stimulate student motivations for reading. Leaders can sponsor/expedite special events reading-related for students. They should periodically participate in student progress monitoring. On occasion, they can personally teach a small student group. They can present students with goals, challenging them to read to attain these. Leaders can also do some of their own reading in classrooms during silent reading periods, so students see them reading.

Culturally relevant instruction

The original definition of culturally relevant instruction, by the scholar who coined the term, is "a pedagogy that empowers students intellectually, socially, emotionally, and politically by using cultural referents to impart knowledge, skills, and attitudes." (Ladson-Billings, 1994) Other scholars call this "culturally appropriate", "culturally congruent", "culturally responsive", and "culturally compatible" instruction. Using culturally relevant teaching enables teachers to build bridges between students' school and home lives, while still fulfilling school district and state curriculum requirements. Culturally relevant instruction uses students' experiences, backgrounds, and knowledge to inform teachers' methods and lessons. Teachers demonstrating outstanding success with instructing diverse students are found to hold fundamental beliefs that all children can succeed, as well as commitment to and pride in their profession. They respect and have fair and flexible relationships with students, frequently showing their support through community event attendance. They believe in developing learner communities in which all students collaborate, sharing responsibility for one another's learning. They teach to and through student strengths. They understand diverse students' needs to function in different worlds.

According to the originator of the term (Ladson-Billings, 1994), culturally relevant teaching should meet three criteria. (1) students experience academic success. This involves not only providing them with tools to achieve academic competence, but also developing student literacy, numeracy, technological, social, and political skills; and motivating students to "choose academic excellence" by emphasizing the real-life significance of academic success. (2) Students must maintain and/or develop cultural competence. Educators must encourage students to preserve their cultural integrity. Many diverse students perceive that they cannot be themselves in school because this setting does not value the student's non-mainstream culture. Culturally relevant teachers use students' cultures as learning vehicles, building curricula upon students' cultural experiences and existing knowledge. (3) Students must develop critical thinking whereby they challenge the social order's status quo. They must learn to criticize cultural values, mores, institutions, and norms that create and sustain social inequalities. Developing these skills may facilitate their acting to effect positive social change. Students must engage in citizenship beyond individual success.

Effectiveness of school's core reading program

For any school reading program, a goal that is perhaps the most important is that it effect continuous achievement by its students. Assessment procedures are included in core programs; these procedures supply teachers with feedback regarding what degrees of mastery students have reached over specific reading skills, particularly for beginning readers. Assessment practices must also identify students in need of more support, practice, and instruction. Legislation and approaches that hold schools and teachers accountable for student reading success dictate that teachers must measure separate indices of student performance to justify their instructional practices in reading. Teachers use student reading outcomes to guide their efforts to assure that all students meet or surpass school district and state standards for levels of reading proficiency and learning. A core reading program can be considered effective if, by the end of the third grade, all but a few students read at grade level; and those few students who are struggling with reading can still achieve some progress as well.

Teachers functioning as resources

Teachers can act as resources for their schools in a multitude of ways. For example, when a teacher tries a particular instructional method, strategy, or technique and finds it effective, rather than simply continuing to use it, s/he can share it with fellow teachers and school administrators. A teacher who has demonstrated superior success in specific areas, such as teaching reading to learning-disabled students or ESL/ELL students, behavior management, or classroom management, can lead in-service trainings to teach other educators his/her methods and techniques. Teachers who know American Sign Language (ASL) can teach it to other educators who are unprepared for a new class including deaf students. Teachers who have found helpful resources for socioeconomically disadvantaged students and their families can disseminate information about these to all school staff. When administrators announce that the school must improve student achievement to meet legal standards, teachers can do research into effective, evidence-based methods and share these for implementation, reducing pressure on everyone involved and providing feelings of relief and hope.

General education vs. special education roles

General education teachers typically are mainly responsible for teaching curriculum that their school system requires to students. Special education teachers typically are mainly responsible for adapting, modifying, and developing methods and materials to fit each student's special needs, strengths, and learning style. Individual student needs frequently determine curriculum in special education. Both general education and special education teachers are trained and experienced in learning processes and instructional techniques. General education teachers contribute specialized expertise in subject-area content; special education teachers contribute specialized expertise in student assessment and instructional adaptations. When the two collaborate in teaching, their goal is that every student in the class receives suitable assignments, and is learning, being challenged, and participating actively in the classroom learning process. Research finds that with disabled and low-achieving students, collaborative teaching promotes better self-images, social skills, peer relationships, motivation, recognition of their own academic and social strengths, and less critical attitudes. Strengthened sense and valuation of self, and appreciation and acceptance of others, result in all students.

Collaborative teaching

Researchers have found that co-teachers who experience success identify five themes as important to teaching collaboratively. (1) Each co-teacher must have confidence in his or her teaching partner's skills. (2) Learning environments should be designed such that they demand active involvement by both the students and the educators. (3) Teachers and others should work to create learning environments wherein each individual's contributions are valued and respected. (4) Teachers need to develop routines that are effective for making it easier for them to conduct in-depth planning of their instruction. (5) Over time, collaborative teachers need to increase their creativity, productivity, and collaboration. Researchers found a consensus of teachers participating in collaborative teaching programs agreed that, while they did not need any less time for planning as the school year continued, the quality of their instruction did continue to improve over the school year. School staff reported to researchers that collaborative instruction afforded improved teaching motivation; personal support; and professional growth, including enhanced instructional preparation, planning, and classroom delivery skills.

Professional development

In research into professional development, participating teachers identified two components that had the greatest influence on their skills and knowledge whereby they changed their teaching practices. An emphasis on content knowledge was the first component. The second was coherence; this entails building upon teachers' existing knowledge. A responsibility of effective professional development is to assist teachers in aligning their instructional content with the school district's and state's standards and assessment procedures. Teacher support from professional development coaches includes encouraging teachers to share with each other their reflections on how they apply the new information they learn to fortifying their teaching practices. Good professional development should provide teachers with information about scientific reading research evidence-based instructional programs, strategies, and materials. It should promote active teacher engagement in skills, planning, and information. Goals of professional development include enabling teachers to use assessment data to direct their teaching; and improving teacher abilities for implementing programs of early intervention and remediation in reading.

Experts recommend that high-quality professional development for educators include such activities as: collaboration among colleagues to analyze assessments and plan instruction at each grade level; collaboration among teachers of different content-area subjects, also for purposes of analyzing assessments and planning instruction; collaboration among specialists in different areas of education, for the same purposes as the previous two activities; modeling of effective instructional practices and behaviors; peer coaching among educators; vertical teaming (i.e. collaboration among colleagues who teaching different grade levels); the formation of book study groups; and the conduction of action research and the sharing of what that research finds. Professional development regarding school core programs typically occurs during summer so that teachers are prepared for the new school year. To prepare teachers for implementing their schools' selected core, supplemental, and intervention programs, professional development should also provide them with program-specific training. All personnel involved, not only teachers, should receive professional development, particularly for school-wide reading programs, because all participants are needed to coordinate objectives, training, and assessments.

Connections

School-home vs.parental involvement for supporting student literacy learning
Federal legislation like the No Child Left Behind (NCLB) Act recognizes parents as children's first teachers. Schools can fortify their reading programs by helping parents understand their rights under NCLB, including enabling their choices of supplemental services if their children's needs are not sufficiently met by the school. One way to give parents training and materials they need to support their children's learning is establishing good school-to-home connections and communications. NCLB mandates U.S. states to provide parents with detailed reports that are easily read about districts, schools, which are successful, and why. Parents can determine whether their school serves all students well via these reports. Other educational acts, including Title I, recognize parental involvement's importance to supporting high student achievement standards. However, the majority of principals in Title I public schools have reported limited parental involvement as an obstacle to applying high

standards. National surveys have found that low-income families are less actively engaged in their children's schools than higher-income families; and that classroom reading averages correlate strongly with parental involvement levels.

<u>Connections between schools, families, and communities relative to students' academic achievement</u>

From synthesizing various research studies, educational development experts have concluded, regardless of income, culture, ethnicity, or race, the majority of families are concerned about their children's success and have high aspirations for them. They also find racial, ethnic, and cultural minority families are engaged actively in their children's education. This engagement can vary from the engagement of "mainstream" white American families. Researchers suggest that the kinds and degrees of family involvement at low-income levels may be attributable to poverty and related economic stressors. Studies also show that schools can frequently help low-income and minority families to become more involved in their children's education by eliminating obstacles, such as language differences; cultural beliefs about family roles in education; issues of exclusion and discrimination; lack of family knowledge/understanding of American educational practices; limitations in time and/or transportation, and child-care needs. From reviewing the literature, experts additionally conclude that concentrating on any single variable is insufficient, and that the complexities of family-community-school interactions must be addressed to eliminate achievement gaps among student populations.

Developing relationships among schools, families, and communities

At the district and school levels, administrators are advised by educational development experts to adopt formal policies to encourage family engagement. This should include a specific emphasis on promoting the involvement of families representing the school population's full diversity. School principals who show ongoing, active support will facilitate family involvement. Schools should outwardly recognize both the differences and similarities among students and their families. All school personnel should respect the hopes and concerns for students of their families. Administrators should initiate training to reinforce school staff's skills in working with families. For immigrant families, schools should provide support to help them understand the workings of American schools, and school expectations of students and their families. School administrators and staff should prioritize community outreach, taking the extra measures that are needed to enable families to become actively involved in their children's educations.

Helping low-income and minority families

Experts in educational development have reviewed multiple research studies into school practices and programs that support our nation's increasingly diverse population. These reviews have resulted in their recommending that for students from low-income and minority families, the schools must furnish their families with early literacy training and resources, and help them to use specific monitoring and communication strategies to support their children's learning in school, at home, and in their community. The experts also believe that the schools should invite minority and low-income students to become engaged in various after-school and extracurricular activities that are sponsored by the community and by the school—and support them. The researchers additionally have pointed out that helping low-income and minority families to procure the community services and support that they need in order to ensure their adequate safety, health, and nutrition can also bolster the academic achievement of their children in school.

Practice Test

Practice Questions

1. Sea and *see*, *fair* and *fare*, are called:
- a. Homophones
- b. Antonyms
- c. Homophobes
- d. Twin words

2. Another name for a persuasive essay is:
- a. Dynamic essay
- b. Convincing essay
- c. Argumentative essay
- d. Position paper

3. A teacher is working with a group of third graders at the same reading level. Her goal is to improve reading fluency. She asks each child in turn to read a page from a book about mammal young. She asks the children to read with expression. She also reminds them they don't need to stop between each word; they should read as quickly as they comfortably can. She cautions them, however, not to read so quickly that they leave out or misread a word. The teacher knows the components of reading fluency are:
- a. Speed, drama, and comprehension
- b. Cohesion, rate, and prosody
- c. Understanding, rate, and prosody

- d. Rate, accuracy, and prosody

4. "Language load" refers to:
- a. The basic vocabulary words a first grader has committed to memory.
- b. The number of unrecognizable words an English Language Learner encounters when reading a passage or listening to a teacher.
- c. The damage that carrying a pile of heavy books could cause to a child's physique.
- d. The number of different languages a person has mastered.

5. A syllable must contain:
- a. A vowel
- b. A consonant
- c. Both a vowel and a consonant
- d. A meaning

- 92 -

6. A third-grade teacher has several students reading above grade level. Most of the remaining students are reading at grade level. There are also a few students reading below grade level. She decides to experiment. Her hypothesis is that by giving the entire class a chapter book above grade level, high-level readers will be satisfied, grade-level readers will be challenged in a positive way, and students reading below grade level will be inspired to improve. Her method is most likely to:
   a. Succeed, producing students reading at an Instructional reading level. High-level readers will be happy to be given material appropriate to their reading level. Grade-level readers will challenge themselves to improve reading strategies in order to master the text. Because only a few of the students are reading below grade level, the other students, who feel happy and energized, will inspire the slower readers by modeling success.
   b. Succeed, producing students reading at an Independent reading level. High-level readers will independently help grade-level readers who will, in turn, independently help those below grade level.
   c. Fail, producing students at a Frustration reading level. Those reading below grade level are likely to give up entirely. Those reading at grade level are likely to get frustrated and form habits that will actually slow down their development.
   d. Fail, producing students reading at a Chaotic reading level. By nature, children are highly competitive. The teacher has not taken into consideration multiple learning styles. The children who are at grade level will either become bitter and angry at those whose reading level is above grade level or simply give up. The children reading below grade level will not be able to keep up and will in all likelihood act out their frustration or completely shut down.

7. Of the three tiers of words, the most important words for direct instruction are:
   a. Tier-one words
   b. Common words
   c. Tier-two words
   d. Words with Latin roots

8. At the beginning of each month, Mr. Yi has Jade read a page or two from a book she hasn't seen before. He notes the total number of words in the section, and also notes the number of times she leaves out or misreads a word. If Jade reads the passage with less than 3% error, Mr. Yi is satisfied that Jade is:
   a. Reading with full comprehension.
   b. Probably bored and should try a more difficult book.
   c. Reading at her Independent reading level.
   d. Comfortable with the syntactical meaning.

9. The purpose of corrective feedback is:
   a. To provide students with methods for explaining to the teacher or classmates what a passage was about.
   b. To correct an error in reading a student has made, specifically clarifying where and how the error was made so that the student can avoid similar errors in the future.
   c. To provide a mental framework that will help the student correctly organize new information.
   d. To remind students that error is essential in order to truly understand and that it is not something to be ashamed of.

10. Dr. Jenks is working with a group of high school students. They are about to read a science book about fossils. Before they begin, she writes the words *stromatolites, fossiliferous,* and *eocene* on the board. She explains the meaning of each word. These words are examples of:

    a.   Academic words
    b.   Alliteration
    c.   Content-specific words
    d.   Ionization

11. Which of the following best explains the importance prior knowledge brings to the act of reading?

    a.   Prior knowledge is information the student gets through researching a topic prior to reading the text. A student who is well-prepared through such research is better able to decode a text and retain its meaning.
    b.   Prior knowledge is knowledge the student brings from previous life or learning experiences to the act of reading. It is not possible for a student to fully comprehend new knowledge without first integrating it with prior knowledge.
    c.   Prior knowledge is predictive. It motivates the student to look for contextual clues in the reading and predict what is likely to happen next.
    d.   Prior knowledge is not important to any degree to the act of reading, because every text is self-contained and therefore seamless. Prior knowledge is irrelevant in this application.

12. A cloze test evaluates a student's:

    a.   Reading fluency.
    b.   Understanding of context and vocabulary.
    c.   Phonemic skills.
    d.   Ability to apply the alphabetic principle to previously unknown material.

13. Sight words are:

    a.   Common words with irregular spelling.
    b.   Words that can easily be found on educational websites.
    c.   Any word that can be seen, including text words, words on signs, brochures, banners, and so forth.
    d.   There is no such thing; because oral language is learned before written language, all words are ultimately based on sound. The correct term is sound words and includes all words necessary to decode a particular text.

14. *Phone, they, church.* The underlined letters in these words are examples of:

    a.   Consonant blend
    b.   Consonant shift
    c.   Continental shift
    d.   Consonant digraph

15. Phonemic awareness is a type of:
   a. Phonological awareness. Phonemic awareness is the ability to recognize sounds within words.
   b. Phonics. It is a teaching technique whereby readers learn the relationship between letters and sounds.
   c. Alphabetization. Unless a reader knows the alphabet, phonemic awareness is useless.
   d. Syntactical awareness. Understanding the underlying structure of a sentence is key to understanding meaning.

16. All members of a group of kindergarten students early in the year are able to chant the alphabet. The teacher is now teaching the students what the alphabet looks like in written form. The teacher points to a letter and the students vocalize the correspondent sound. Alternatively, the teacher vocalizes a phoneme and a student points to it on the alphabet chart. The teacher is using _____ in her instruction.
   a. Letter–sound correspondence
   b. Rote memorization
   c. Predictive analysis
   d. Segmentation

17. A fourth-grade teacher is preparing her students for a reading test in which a number of words have been replaced with blanks. The test will be multiple-choice; there are three possible answers given for each blank. The teacher instructs the children to read all the possible answers and cross out any answer that obviously doesn't fit. Next, the students should "plug in" the remaining choices and eliminate any that are grammatically incorrect or illogical. Finally, the student should consider contextual clues in order to select the best answer. This in an example of:
   a. Strategy instruction
   b. Diagnostic instruction
   c. Skills instruction
   d. Multiple-choice instruction

18. The term "common words" means:
   a. One-syllable words with fewer than three letters. Some examples are it, an, a, I, go, to, and in. They are the first words an emergent writer learns.
   b. One-syllable words with fewer than five letters. Some examples include sing, goes, sit, rock, walk, and took.
   c. Words that are ordinary or unexceptional; because they tend to flatten a piece of writing, they should be avoided.
   d. Familiar, frequently used words that do not need to be taught beyond primary grades.

19. Which is greater, the number of English phonemes or the number of letters in the alphabet?
   a. The number of letters in the alphabet, because they can be combined to create phonemes.
   b. The number of phonemes. A phoneme is the smallest measure of language sound.
   c. They are identical; each letter "owns" a correspondent sound.
   d. Neither. Phonemes and alphabet letters are completely unrelated.

20. *Train, brain, spring.* The underlined letters are examples of:
  a. Consonant digraph
  b. Consonant blend
  c. Consonant shift
  d. Continental shift

21. It is the beginning of the school year. To determine which second-grade students might need support, the reading teacher wants to identify those who are reading below grade level. She works with students one at a time. She gives each child a book at a second-grade reading level and asks the child to read out loud for two minutes. Children who will need reading support are those who read:
  a. Fewer than 100 words in the time given.
  b. Fewer than 200 words in the time given.
  c. More than 75 words in the time given.
  d. The entire book in the time given.

22. The most effective strategy for decoding sight words is:
  a. Segmenting sight words into syllables. Beginning readers are understandably nervous when encountering a long word that isn't familiar. Blocking off all but a single syllable at a time renders a word manageable and allows the reader a sense of control over the act of reading.
  b. Word families. By grouping the sight word with similar words, patterns emerge.
  c. A phonemic approach. When students understand the connection between individual words and their sounds, they will be able to sound out any sight word they encounter.
  d. None; sight words cannot be decoded. Readers must learn to recognize these words as wholes on sight.

23. The reading teacher is working with a group of English Language Learners. Which of the following strategies will help these students learn to read with enhanced fluency?
  a. The teacher reads aloud while students follow the words in their books.
  b. Tape-assisted reading.
  c. Having the students' parents or another trustworthy adult read with the child each evening for 45 minutes.
  d. A and B.

24. "Decoding" is also called:
  a. Remediation
  b. Deciphering
  c. Alphabetic principle
  d. Deconstruction

25. A reading teacher is working with a group of English Language Learners. She has asked them to study sequentially the pictures in a storybook and then tell her what they think the story is about. This approach will help the students understand the _____ of the story.
  a. Theme
  b. Context
  c. Events
  d. Deeper meaning

- 96 -

26. Phonological awareness activities are:
    a. Oral
    b. Visual
    c. Both A and B
    d. Semantically based

27. A student is able to apply strategies to comprehend the meanings of unfamiliar words; can supply definitions for words with several meanings such as *crucial, criticism,* and *witness*; and is able to reflect on her background knowledge in order to decipher a word's meaning. These features of effective reading belong to which category?
    a. Word recognition
    b. Vocabulary
    c. Content
    d. Comprehension

28. A reading teacher is assessing an eighth grader to determine her reading level. Timed at a minute, the student reads with 93% accuracy. She misreads an average of seven words out of 100. What is her reading level?
    a. She is reading at a Frustration level.
    b. She is reading at an Excellence level.
    c. She is reading at an Instructional level.
    d. She is reading at an Independent level.

29. When should students learn how to decode?
    a. Decoding is the most basic and essential strategy to becoming a successful reader. It should be introduced to kindergartners during the first two weeks of school.
    b. Decoding is not a teachable skill. It is an unconscious act and is natural to all learners.
    c. Decoding should be taught only after children have mastered every letter–sound relationship as well as every consonant digraph and consonant blend. They should also be able to recognize and say the 40 phonemes common to English words and be able to recognize at least a dozen of the most common sight words.
    d. Decoding depends on an understanding of letter–sound relationships. As soon as a child understands enough letters and their correspondent sounds to read a few words, decoding should be introduced.

30. *Since, whether,* and *accordingly* are examples of which type of signal words?
    a. Common, or basic, signal words
    b. Compare/contrast words
    c. Cause–effect words
    d. Temporal sequencing words

31. A class is reading *The Heart Is a Lonely Hunter*. The teacher asks students to write a short paper explaining the story's resolution. She is asking them to locate and discuss the story's:
    a. Outcome
    b. Highest or most dramatic moment
    c. Plot
    d. Lowest point

32. A student encounters a multisyllabic word. She's not sure if she's seen it before. What should she do first? What should she do next?
   a. Locate familiar word parts, then locate the consonants.
   b. Locate the consonants, then locate the vowels.
   c. Locate the vowels, then locate familiar word parts.
   d. Look it up in the dictionary, then write down the meaning.

READ THE FOLLOWING STORY, THEN ANSWER THE QUESTIONS THAT FOLLOW:

The kindergarten teacher is concerned about three of her students. While they are enthusiastic about writing, they do not always recognize letters, confusing b, d, and p, or e and o. They do, however, know which sounds go with certain letters when they are orally drilled. When they write, they appear to be attempting letter–sound associations.

"Now I'm writing *M*," the teacher heard one boy say as he scripted a large *N* in the upper right corner of his paper. He studied it for a moment and added, "Nope, it needs another leg." The student then wrote an *I* beside the *N*. "There," he said. "Now you are an *M*. I can write the word, 'man,' because now I have *M*." The child then moved to the lower left corner of the paper. "M-A-N," he said to himself, slowly pronouncing each sound. "I already have that *M*. Here is where the rest of the word goes." He turned the paper sideways and wrote *N*.

The second child sang to herself as she gripped the crayon and scribbled lines here and there on her paper. Some of the lines resembled letters, but few actually were. Others were scribbles. As she "wrote," she seemed to be making up a story and seemed to believe she was writing the story down.

The third child didn't vocalize at all while he worked. He gripped the paper and carefully wrote the same letter over and over and over. Sometimes the letter was large, sometimes tiny. He turned the paper in every direction so that sometimes the letter was sideways or upside down. Sometimes he flipped it backward. "What are you writing?" the teacher asked him. "My name," the child told her. The teacher then realized the letter was, indeed, the first letter of his name. She gently told him he had done a fine job of writing the first letter of his name. Did he want her to help him write the rest of it? "Nope," he cheerfully told her, "it's all here." He pointed at one of the letters and "read" his full name. He pointed at another letter and again seemed to believe it represented all the sounds of his name.

33. The kindergarten teacher isn't certain if these children are exhibiting signs of a reading disability or other special needs. What should the teacher do?

    a. Nothing. These children are simply at an early stage in the reading/writing process.

    b. Nothing. She doesn't want to have to tell the parents that their children are sub-par in terms of intelligence. They are perfectly nice children and can contribute to society in other ways. She resolves to give them extra attention in other areas to help them build confidence.

    c. She should recommend that the parents take the children to be tested for a number of reading disorders, including dyslexia.

    d. She should arrange a meeting between herself, the school psychologist, and the reading specialist to discuss the matter and resolve it using a three-pronged approach.

34. In the above example, the emergent writers are demonstrating their understanding that letters symbolize predictable sounds, that words begin with an initial sound/letter, and that by "writing," they are empowering themselves by offering a reader access to their thoughts and ideas. The next three stages the emergent writers will pass through in order will most likely be:

    a. Scripting the end-sound to a word (KT=cat); leaving space between words; writing from the top left to the top right of the page, and from top to bottom.

    b. Scripting the end-sound to a word (KT=cat); writing from the top left to the top right of the page, and from top to bottom; separating the words from one another with a space between.

    c. Leaving space between the initial letters that represent words; writing from the top left to the top right of the page, and from top to bottom; scripting the final sound of each word as well as the initial sound (KT=cat).

    d. Drawing a picture beside each of the initial sounds to represent the entire word; scripting the end-sound to a word (KT=cat); scripting the interior sounds that compose the entire word (KAT=cat).

35. The teacher might best encourage the three students in the above example by:

    a. Suggesting they write an entire book rather than just a single page. This will build confidence, teach them sequencing, and encourage the young writers to delve deeper into their ideas.

    b. Ask the students to read their stories to her. Suggest they visit other children in the class and read to each of them.

    c. Contact the local newspaper and invite a reporter to visit her class and write a story about her emergent writers. In this way, they are sure to see themselves as "real writers" and will more fully apply themselves to the task.

    d. Invite all the parents to visit the class the following week. This will give all classmates, regardless of where they are on the learning spectrum, time to memorize their stories. The children will be very excited and will begin to see themselves as "real writers."

36. At what point should the kindergarten teacher in the above example offer the three children picture books and ask them to read to her?
   a. When the three children are all able to script initial sounds, end sounds, and interior sounds they are ready to decode words. She should make her request at this point.
   b. As each child reaches the stage in which he or she can script initial sounds, end sounds, and interior sounds, the teacher should ask only that child to read to her.
   c. As each child reaches the stage in which he habitually writes from the top to the bottom of the page, moving left to right, the time has come. Books are intended to be read in this way, and until a child has had the experience of writing in the same manner, he won't be able to make sense of the words.
   d. The teacher should encourage all students to "read" picture books from the first day of school. Talking about the pictures from page to page gives young readers the idea that books are arranged sequentially. Pictures also offer narrative coherence and contextual clues. Emergent readers who are encouraged to enjoy books will more readily embrace the act of reading. Holding a book and turning pages gives young readers a familiarity with them.

37. How does a teacher most effectively teach spelling?
   a. Students who have a clear understanding of letter–sound association do not need to be taught to spell. If they can say a word, they can spell it.
   b. Students who have a clear understanding of letter–sound association, who can identify syllables, and who recognize when the base word is of Latin, Greek, or Indo-European ancestry do not need to be taught to spell. They can deduce what is most likely the correct spelling using a combination of these strategies. A teacher who posts charts organizing words into their ancestor families, phonemic units, and word-sound families is efficiently teaching spelling. The rest is up to the student.
   c. Students who spell poorly will be at a disadvantage for the rest of their lives. It is essential that students spend at least 15 minutes a day drilling spelling words until they know them forward and backward. The teacher should alternate between having students write a new word 25 times and having the entire class chant the spelling of the words.
   d. Students should be taught that writing is a process. By teaching students to apply spelling patterns found in common phonemic units, the spelling of many words can be deduced. Sight words that are high frequency and do not follow patterns found in other words (the, guardian, colonel) must be taught.

38. A teacher is teaching students analogizing. She is teaching them to:
   a. Identify and use metaphors.
   b. Identify and use similes.
   c. Identify and use groups of letters that occur in a word family.
   d. Identify and use figures of speech.

39. A reading teacher is working with a student who has just moved to Texas from Korea. The child knows very few words in English. The teacher offers her a picture book of Korean folk tales. Using words and gestures, the teacher asks her to "read" one folk tale. The child "reads" the familiar tale in Korean. The teacher then writes key English words on the board and asks the child to find those words in the book. When the child finds the words, they read them together. This strategy is:
   a. Useful. The child will feel more confident because the story is already familiar. She will also feel that the lesson is a conversation of sorts, and that she is communicating successfully. She will be motivated to learn the English words because they are meaningful and highly charged.
   b. Useful. The teacher is learning as much as the child is. The teacher is learning about Korean culture and language, and she can apply this knowledge when teaching future Korean students.
   c. Not very useful. The child needs to be exposed to as much American culture as possible. Encouraging her to remember her own culture will make her sad and will limit her curiosity about her new home.
   d. Not very useful. The first things the child should learn are the letters of the alphabet and associative sounds. Only then can she begin to decipher an unfamiliar language.

40. The teacher in the previous question was using what kind of load?
   a. Language load
   b. Cognitive load
   c. Bilingual load
   d. Cultural load

41. Using brain imaging, researchers have discovered that dyslexic readers use the _____ side(s) of their brains, while non-dyslexic readers use the _____ side(s) of their brains.
   a. Left; right
   b. Right; left
   c. Right and left; left
   d. Right; left and right

42. A fifth grader has prepared a report on reptiles, which is something he knows a great deal about. He rereads his report and decides to make a number of changes. He moves a sentence from the top to the last paragraph. He crosses out several words and replaces them with more specific words. He circles key information and draws an arrow to show another place the information could logically be placed. He is engaged in:
   a. Editing
   b. Revising
   c. First editing, then revising
   d. Reviewing

43. *Bi, re,* and *un* are:
   a. Suffixes, appearing at the beginning of base words to change their meaning.
   b. Suffixes, appearing at the end of base words to enhance their meaning.
   c. Prefixes, appearing at the beginning of base words to emphasize their meaning.
   d. Prefixes, appearing at the beginning of base words to change their meanings.

44. Examples of CVC words include:
   a. Add, pad, mad
   b. Cat, tack, act
   c. Elephant, piano, examine
   d. Dog, sit, leg

45. A teacher is working with a student who is struggling with reading. The teacher gives him a story with key words missing:

   The boy wanted to take the dog for a walk. The boy opened the door. The ____ ran out. The ___ looked for the dog. When he found the dog, he was very _____.

The student is able to fill in the blanks by considering:
   a. Syntax. Oftentimes, word order gives enough clues that a reader can predict what happens next.
   b. Pretext. By previewing the story, the student can deduce the missing words.
   c. Context. By considering the other words in the story, the student can determine the missing words.
   d. Sequencing. By putting the ideas in logical order, the student can determine the missing words.

46. The following is/are (an) element(s) of metacognition:
   a. A reader's awareness of herself as a learner.
   b. A reader's understanding of a variety of reading strategies and how to apply them to comprehend a text.
   c. A reader who is conscious about remembering what has been read.
   d. All of the above.

47. Collaborative Strategic Reading (CSR) is a teaching technique that depends on two teaching practices. These practices are:
   a. Cooperative learning and reading comprehension.
   b. Cooperative reading and metacognition.
   c. Reading comprehension and metacognition.
   d. Cooperative learning and metacognition.

48. Context cues are useful in:
   a. Predicting future action.
   b. Understanding the meaning of words that are not familiar.
   c. Understanding character motivation.
   d. Reflecting on a text's theme.

49. A teacher has a child who does not volunteer in class. When the teacher asks the student a question the student can answer, she does so with as few words as possible. The teacher isn't sure how to best help the child. She should:
   a. Leave the child alone. She is clearly very shy and will be embarrassed by having attention drawn to her. She is learning in her own way.
   b. Ask two or three highly social children to include this girl in their activities. She is shy, and she probably won't approach them on her own.
   c. Observe the child over the course of a week or two. Draw her into conversation and determine if her vocabulary is limited, if she displays emotional problems, or if her reticence could have another cause. Note how the child interacts with others in the class. Does she ever initiate conversation? If another child initiates, does she respond?
   d. Refer her to the school counselor immediately. It is clear the child is suffering from either a low IQ or serious problems at home.

50. A first grader is reading a book aloud. The teacher notes that the book uses word families. Some of the words are *fat, hat, sat, fit, hit, sit, run, fun, sun, hot, cot,* and *not.* The child ignores the pictures and attempts to read by identifying the rhyme. However, she frequently misreads, replacing the correct word with another from the same word family. The child needs:
   a. Encouragement. She will eventually understand.
   b. Intervention. She can identify groups of letters, but is not able to apply letter–sound association.
   c. To practice singing the alphabet.
   d. Nothing. This is a normal stage in the reading process.

51. A high school class reads an essay about the possible effects of sexual activity on teens. The author's position is very clear: She believes young people should avoid sex because they aren't mature enough to take the necessary steps to remain safe. The author cites facts, research studies, and statistics to strengthen her position. This type of writing is called:
   a. Expository
   b. Narrative
   c. Persuasive
   d. Didactic

52. A reading teacher feels that some of his strategies aren't effective. He has asked a specialist to observe him and make suggestions as to how he can improve. The reading specialist should suggest that first:
   a. The teacher set up a video camera and record several sessions with different students for the specialist to review. The presence of an observer changes the outcome; if the specialist is in the room, it will negatively affect the students' ability to read.
   b. The teacher reflect on his strategies himself. Which seem to work? Which don't? Can the teacher figure out why? It's always best to encourage teachers to find their own solutions so that they can handle future issues themselves.
   c. They meet to discuss areas the teacher is most concerned about and decide on the teacher's goals.
   d. The specialist should arrive unannounced to observe the teacher interacting with students. This will prevent the teacher from unconsciously overpreparing.

53. A kindergarten teacher pronounces a series of word pairs for her students. The students repeat the pairs. Some of the pairs rhyme (*see/bee*) and some of the pairs share initial sounds but do not rhyme (*sit, sun*). The students help her separate the word pairs into pairs that rhyme and pairs that do not. Once the students are able to distinguish between two words that rhyme and two words that do not, the teacher says a word and asks them to provide a rhyme. When she says *cat* a child responds with *fat*. When she says *sing* a child offers *thing*. How does this strictly oral activity contribute to the children's ability to read?
   a. It doesn't. Oral activities must have a written component to be useful to emergent readers.
   b. It is helpful in that it demonstrates how different sounds are made with different letters.
   c. It actually discourages children from reading. By emphasizing orality over literacy, the teacher is suggesting to the children that reading is not an important skill.
   d. Being able to identify rhyme is an important element of phonological awareness.

54. Syllable types include:
   a. Closed, open, silent e, vowel team, vowel-r, and consonant-le.
   b. Closed, open, silent, double-vowel, r, and le.
   c. Closed, midway, open, emphasized, prefixed, and suffixed.
   d. Stressed, unstressed, and silent.

55. An eighth-grade student is able to decode most words fluently and has a borderline/acceptable vocabulary, but his reading comprehension is quite low. He can be helped with instructional focus on:
   a. Strategies to increase comprehension and to build vocabulary.
   b. Strategies to increase comprehension and to be able to identify correct syntactical usage.
   c. Strategies to improve his understanding of both content and context.
   d. Strategies to build vocabulary and to improve his understanding of both content and context.

56. Reading comprehension and vocabulary can best be assessed:
   a. With brief interviews and tests every two months to determine how much learning has taken place. Students learn in spurts, and in-depth assessments of comprehension and vocabulary are a waste of time.
   b. Through a combination of standardized testing, informal teacher observations, attention to grades, objective-linked assessments, and systematized charting of data over time.
   c. By giving students weekly self-assessment rubrics to keep them constantly aware of and invested in their own progress.
   d. By having students retell a story or summarize the content of an informational piece of writing. The degree to which the material was comprehended, and the richness or paucity of vocabulary used in such work, provides efficient and thorough assessment.

57. An ORF is:
   a. An Oral Reading Fluency assessment.
   b. An Occasional Reading Function assessment.
   c. An Oscar Reynolds Feinstein assessment.
   d. An Overt Reading Failure assessment.

58. An outcome assessment is given:
   a. At the end of the year, to determine if instructional goals established at the beginning of the year have been successfully reached.
   b. At the beginning of the year to establish a point of reference for a series of regularly administered assessments throughout the year.
   c. When a student has finished a text to determine how clearly she understood the story's implied outcome.
   d. There is no such assessment.

59. Word-recognition ability is:
   a. Equally important to all readers.
   b. Used only by fluent readers.
   c. Another term for "word attack."
   d. Especially important to English Language Learners and students with reading disabilities.

60. Research indicates that developing oral language proficiency in emergent readers is important because:
   a. Proficiency with oral language enhances students' phonemic awareness and increases vocabulary.
   b. The more verbally expressive emergent readers are, the more confident they become. Such students will embrace both Academic and Independent reading levels.
   c. It encourages curiosity about others. With strong oral language skills, students begin to question the world around them. The more they ask, the richer their background knowledge.
   d. It demonstrates to students that their ideas are important and worth sharing.

61. In preparation for writing a paper, a high school class has been instructed to skim a number of Internet and print documents. They are being asked to:
   a. Read the documents several times, skimming to a deeper level of understanding each time.
   b. Read the documents quickly, looking for those that offer the most basic, general information.
   c. Read the documents quickly, looking for key words in order to gather the basic premise of each.
   d. Read the documents carefully, looking for those that offer the most in-depth information.

62. The students in the above question are most likely preparing to write a(n) _____ essay:
   a. Personal
   b. Expository
   c. Literary
   d. Narrative

A TEACHER HAS GIVEN THE FIRST PARAGRAPH OF AN ESSAY TO HER STUDENTS TO ANALYZE AND DISCUSS. READ THE PARAGRAPH AND ANSWER THE FOLLOWING QUESTIONS:

Americans have struggled with cigarettes far too long. Until now, it has been a personal choice to smoke (or not), but the time for change is rapidly approaching. Local legislation has already begun for schools, restaurants, arenas, and other public places to be smoke-free. Years ago cigarette smoking was presented by the media as being fashionable, even sexy. In magazines, movies, and later in television, celebrities would indulge themselves with a smoke and even be paid to endorse a brand. As recently as 1975, it was common for talk show hosts like Tom Snyder and Johnny Carson to keep a cigarette burning. Cigarette smoking in America has persisted in spite of frightening concerns like lung cancer and emphysema. Over the years, the tobacco industry has sought to diffuse strong evidence that smoking is harmful. However, the myth of "safe cigarettes," questions about nicotine addiction, and denials about the dangers of secondhand smoke have proven to be propaganda and lies.

63. This is a(n) _____ essay:
    a. Compare/contrast
    b. Persuasive
    c. Narrative
    d. Analytic

64. The thesis statement is:
    a. However, the myth of "safe cigarettes," questions about nicotine addiction, and denials about the dangers of secondhand smoke have proven to be propaganda and lies.
    b. Americans have struggled with cigarettes far too long.
    c. Until now, it has been a personal choice to smoke (or not), but the time for change is rapidly approaching.
    d. In magazines, movies, and later in television, celebrities would indulge themselves with a smoke and even be paid to endorse a brand.

65. The next three paragraphs in the essay will most likely address:
    a. Smoking as a personal choice, changes in local legislation, and how fashionable smoking once was.
    b. How fashionable smoking once was, talk show hosts smoking on air, the myth of "safe cigarettes."
    c. Propaganda and lies, the myth of "safe cigarettes," and how long Americans have struggled with cigarettes.
    d. The myth of "safe cigarettes," questions about nicotine addiction, and the dangers of secondhand smoke.

66. The teacher and her students brainstorm a list of talents, skills, and specialized knowledge belonging to members of the class. Some of the items on the list include how to make a soufflé, how to juggle, and how to teach a dog to do tricks. One student knows a great deal about spiders, and another about motorcycles. She asks each student to write an essay about something he or she is good at or knows a great deal about. What kind of essay is she asking the students to produce?
   a. Cause and effect
   b. Compare/contrast
   c. Example
   d. Argumentative

67. *Caret, carrot, to, two and too* share something in common. They:
   a. Are nouns.
   b. Are monosyllabic.
   c. Are homophones.
   d. Represent things in nature.

READ THE FOLLOWING PARAGRAPH, THEN ANSWER THE QUESTIONS THAT FOLLOW:

A class will visit an assisted living facility to interview residents about their lives. Each group of three has selected a theme such as love, work, or personal accomplishment and written several questions around that theme. Next, each group practices interviewing one another. The teacher then asks all the students to discuss the questions that caused them to respond most thoughtfully, as well as those they were less inspired by. The students decided the questions that were easiest to respond to asked for very specific information; for example, one inspiring question was, "Please tell me about something you learned to do as a child that affected the direction of your life." Those that were uninspiring were too broad, for example, "Please tell me about your happiest memory."

68. After they interview the residents, each group of three students will work together to write a piece about the resident. This kind of approach is called:
   a. Collaborative learning
   b. Companion learning
   c. Bonded learning
   d. Group learning

69. The genre the teacher expects is:
   a. Memoir
   b. Historical fiction
   c. Biography
   d. Autobiography

70. The teacher wants the students to apply what they've learned across content areas. Which of the following strategies would be most effective?
   a. Students will interview a family member, asking the same questions.
   b. Students will write a personal piece in which they address the same questions.
   c. Students will do online research about the cultural, economic, or political events that were occurring during the specific time about which they've written.
   d. Students pretend to be the interviewee and rewrite the piece from a first person point of view.

READ THE FOLLOWING PARAGRAPH, THEN RESPOND TO THE QUESTIONS THAT FOLLOW.

A seventh-grade teacher asks the reading teacher to suggest a lesson students will find simultaneously challenging and fun. The reading teacher suggests the class read fairy tales from both Hans Christian Anderson and the Brothers Grimm and have a rapid-paced, energetic discussion about the many similarities and differences between the two while the teacher lists them on the board.

71. The individual strategies the students will employ are:
    a. Collaborative learning and genre.
    b. Brainstorming and a compare/contrast strategy.
    c. Collaborative learning and brainstorming.
    d. Analyzing and genre.

72. The lesson is asking the students to consider two different:
    a. Learning styles
    b. Genres
    c. Writing styles
    d. Reading styles

73. The primary benefit of this exercise is that it promotes students':
    a. Vocabulary
    b. Comprehension
    c. Fluency
    d. Word identification

74. The students enjoyed the assignment so much that the teacher suggested they select one fairy tale and modernize it without changing the basic structure. Evil kings and queens could become corrupt politicians; pumpkins could turn into Hummers, and romantic princes might reveal themselves as rock stars. The teacher believes this assignment will most effectively demonstrate to the students:
    a. The importance of setting to meaning.
    b. The importance of characters to meaning.
    c. The importance of culture to meaning.
    d. The importance of creativity to meaning.

75. The first-grade teacher wants her class to understand that stories have a certain order. She reads them a story, then orally reviews with them how each event that happened in the story caused the next event to happen. To reinforce the lesson the teacher should:
   a. Give each child a piece of drawing paper that has been folded in half and then again, creating four boxes, along with a piece that has not been folded. The teacher should then ask the students to draw a cartoon about the story. Each of the first four boxes will show the events in order. The second page is to show how the story ends.
   b. Give each child a piece of drawing paper and ask the students to draw the most important scene.
   c. Give each child a piece of drawing paper and ask the students to draw the story's beginning on the front of the page and ending on the back.
   d. Give each child a piece of drawing paper that has been folded in half and then again, creating four boxes, along with a piece that has not been folded. The teacher should then ask the students to draw a cartoon about anything they want. She reminds them to put their story cartoons in proper order.

76. A ninth grade class is reading a 14-line poem in iambic pentameter. There are three stanzas of four lines each, and a two-line couplet at the end. Words at the end of each line rhyme with another word in the same stanza. The class is reading a:
   a. Sonnet
   b. Villanelle
   c. Sestina
   d. Limerick

77. A teacher is working with a group of English Language Learners. She asks them to take two pieces of paper. At the top of the first paper they are to write *SAME*. At the top of the other, *DIFFERENT*. Each child will consider what his native country and the United States have in common, and what distinct features each country possesses. The children are using which method in organizing their ideas?
   a. Hunt and peck
   b. Consider and persuade
   c. Evaluate and contrast
   d. Compare and contrast

78. Next, the teacher in the previous story drew two overlapping circles on the board. She labeled one circle *MALI*. The other circle was labeled *U.S.* She labeled the overlap joining the two circles *SAME*. On the far side of each circle, she wrote *DIFFERENT*. In the *U.S.* circle, she wrote *many cars, very good roads, people live in big cities, many families have pets,* and *houses made of wood.* In the side labeled *MALI* she wrote *fewer cars, many broken roads, most people live in villages, animals are not pets,* and *houses made of mud.* What will she write in the third, overlapping area?
   a. Telephones, personal computers, cars, and apartment buildings.
   b. Dogs, cats, fish, and birds.
   c. People celebrate marriages, births, and historical events.
   d. Movies, *television, books*, and *Internet.*

79. What type of prewriting activity has the teacher in the previous example drawn on the board?
   a. A verbal diagram
   b. Thought bubbles
   c. A web
   d. A Venn diagram

80. A third grader knows he needs to write from left to right, and from top to bottom on the page. He knows what sounds are associated with specific letters. He can recognize individual letters and can hear word families. He correctly identifies prefixes, suffixes, and homonyms, and his reading comprehension is very good. However, when he is asked to write, he becomes very upset. He has trouble holding a pencil, his letters are very primitively executed, and his written work is not legible. He most likely has:
   a. Dysgraphia
   b. Dyslexia
   c. Dyspraxia
   d. Nonverbal learning disorder

81. The phrase "Pretty as a picture" is *best* described as a:
   a. Metaphor
   b. Cliché
   c. Simile
   d. Figure of speech

82. A fourth-grade teacher had her students write haiku in order to promote the students'
_____.
   a. Reading comprehension
   b. Vocabulary
   c. Word identification skills
   d. Confidence

83. A second-grade teacher wants to help her students enrich their vocabulary. She's noticed that their writing journals are filled with serviceable but unexciting verbs such as "said" and "went," and general rather than specific nouns. The most effective lesson would involve:
   a. Suggesting students use a thesaurus to substitute more unusual words for common ones.
   b. Suggesting students add an adjective to each noun.
   c. Brainstorming a list of verbs that mean ways of talking or ways of going, then adding them to the word wall along with some nouns that specify common topics.
   d. Suggesting students look up the meanings of boring words and consider another way to express them.

84. At the beginning of the school year, a parent is concerned about her first-grade child. The child has a very good speaking vocabulary, but this is not reflected in her writing. She reads a little above grade level, but the parent feels the child "fakes it" by looking at the pictures and guessing based on the context of the story. The parent is concerned that the child is not reading so much as remembering what a book is about and filling in areas of confusion with guesses. The parent points to the child's writing samples as further evidence. The day before, the child scripted:

My famble will go to the fare on Saturday we will ride the farus will. We will eat popzikls. I want to win a stuft aminul. (*My family will go to the fair on Saturday. We will ride the Ferris wheel. We will eat popsicles. I want to win a stuffed animal.*)

The teacher:
   a. Shares the parent's concern. They meet with the resource teacher to set up a program to address the problems.
   b. Advocates a wait-and-see policy. It is very early in the school year, and young children often demonstrate very rapid growth in previously problematic areas.
   c. Explains to the parent that the child is not experiencing problems. She is correctly using the sight words she has learned, applying her knowledge of word families to determine spelling of similar words, and correctly hearing phonemes and scripting the words that represent them. Her strong verbal vocabulary and her reading skills are further evidence she is doing well. Her writing will catch up as she learns further strategies and sight words.
   d. Explains to the parent that the child is not experiencing problems. She is eager to memorize sight words, and the teacher feels certain that the student's writing will radically improve as she memorizes the correct the spellings of all the words she wants to write.

85. Examples of onomatopoeia are:
   a. Sink, drink, mink, link.
   b. Their, there, they're.
   c. Drip, chirp, splash, giggle.
   d. *Think, in, thin, ink.*

86. "Code knowledge" facilitates reading fluency because:
   a. It brings the entirety of the student's previous experience to bear on decoding a text.
   b. It offers a framework for organizing new information by assigning code words to sets of ideas.
   c. There is no such thing as "code knowledge." The correct term is "core knowledge."
   d. It offers a systematic approach to untangling the wide variety of vowel sounds when an unfamiliar word is encountered.

87. The purpose of "targeted instruction" is to:
   a. Deliver instructions that are precise, clear, and direct so that students understand exactly what is expected.
   b. Accurately rank a group of learners from low achievers to high achievers so that the teacher knows from the beginning of the school year which students have less ability and will therefore need support.
   c. Teach students how to take information from a text and reorganize it into bulleted lists.
   d. Assess and target areas needing improvement as well as areas of greatest strength for each student to ensure that all members of a class are receiving instruction tailored to their specific needs.

88. Components of "explicit instruction" include:
   a. Clarifying the goal, modeling strategies, and offering explanations geared to a student's level of understanding.
   b. Determining the goal, offering strategies, and asking questions designed to ascertain whether understanding has been reached.
   c. Reassessing the goal, developing strategies, and determining whether further reassessing of the goal is required.
   d. Objectifying the goal, assessing strategies, and offering explanations geared toward a student's level of understanding.

89. A teacher has challenged a student with a book about Antarctica that is just beyond the high end of the student's Instructional level. The teacher points out that the student already knows quite a bit about penguins because the class studied them earlier in the year. He reminds the student that she's recently seen a television show about the seals that also live in Antarctic waters. The teacher gives the student a list of words she's likely to find in the text, and they discuss what those words might mean. The student begins to read, but stops to ask the teacher what *circumpolar* means. The teacher is also unfamiliar with the word, but reminds her that *circum* is a prefix. The student recalls that it means "about or around" and deduces that circumpolar most likely refers to something found around or in a polar region. This instructional approach is called:
   a. Modular instruction
   b. Scaffolding
   c. Linking
   d. Transmutation

90. The second graders are confused. They've learned to hear and count syllables. They understand that contractions such as *won't, didn't,* and *we're* represent two words converted into one. Now the teacher is trying to explain compound words. She has shown the children that a compound word is made of two words and has a meaning that is a little different from either of words that compose it. She pronounces *doghouse,* and asks if it is one word or two. "Two," the students correctly respond. The teacher now says *parent.* Again, the students tell her it's two words. The teacher explains there are two syllables but not two words. One child nods and says, "Like the word 'didn't.' That's two words but it sounds like one." What is the best way for the teacher to correct the students' misunderstanding?

- a. Point out compound words the children use throughout the day. Write them on the board, and ask students to list them in their writing journals.
- b. Assess the degree of confusion. Give the students a quiz listing a number of two-syllable words, compound words, and contractions. Ask the students to cross out the two-syllable words and contractions.
- c. Write a compound word such as doghouse on the board. Underline dog, and then house. Beneath the words draw a picture of a dog and a house, joined with a plus sign. Next, write another compound word and ask the class to draw the pictures in their journals. Give the students a handout with several compound words. Ask them to underline the two words, then to draw the pictures.
- d. Turn the lesson into fun by suggesting the students invent new compound words. Demonstrate by inventing one such as nosemitten instead of scarf. Children learn more readily when they are enjoying it.

91. An understanding of the meanings of prefixes and suffixes such as *dis, mis, un, re, able,* and *ment* are important for:

- a. Reading comprehension
- b. Word recognition
- c. Vocabulary building
- d. Reading fluency

92. VC, CVC, CCVC, CVCC, and CCVCC are among the types of:

- a. Homophones
- b. Closed syllables
- c. Monosyllabic words
- d. Polyglotal indicators

93. A student is taking a reading test. The teacher has blocked out a number of words. Each blank is assigned a set of three possible words. The student must select the correct word from each set so that the text makes sense. The student is taking:

- a. A cloze test
- b. A maze test
- c. A multiple-choice quiz
- d. A vocabulary test

94. When working with English Language Learners, the teacher should:
   a. Avoid idioms and slang, involve students in hands-on activities, reference students' prior knowledge, and speak slowly.
   b. Speak slowly, use monosyllabic words whenever possible, repeat each sentence three times before moving to the next sentence, and employ idioms but not slang.
   c. Use monosyllabic words whenever possible, repeat key instructions three times but not in a row, reference students' prior knowledge, and have students keep a journal of new vocabulary.
   d. Have students keep a journal of new vocabulary, reference students' prior knowledge, speak slowly, and involve students in hands-on activities.

95. Editing involves:
   a. Correcting surface features such as sentence fragments, spelling, and punctuation.
   b. Fine-tuning the underlying structure of the piece to make the theme stand out.
   c. Reconsidering ideas, adding or subtracting information, and changing the underlying structure.
   d. Adding illustrations, charts, and other useful addenda.

96. A seventh grader has never had much success with reading. Her ability to decode is rudimentary; she stops and starts when reading, frequently loses her place, or misreads an important word. She doesn't seem aware of where errors occur, or she does not attempt to correct them. When asked to tell about what she's read, her comprehension is minimal. To help her, instructional focus on which of the following would be most useful?
   a. Carefully organized lessons in decoding, sight words, vocabulary, and comprehension at least three to five times a week. These mini-lessons must be extremely clear, with the parts broken down to the lowest common denominator. The more tightly interwoven and systematized the instruction, the better chance this student will have.
   b. A weekly lesson focusing on one aspect of reading. This student will be overwhelmed if too many strategies are offered at once. The instruction should focus first on recognizing sight words, then letter–sound association. Next, the girl needs an understanding of the rules of syntax.
   c. The student isn't trying. Her instruction should be aimed at helping her learn to be self-motivated and disciplined in her approach to learning.
   d. Comprehension strategies will help her grasp the overall meaning of a text. From there she can begin to drill down until she's able to combine various approaches that, working together, will enable her to read.

97. Silent reading fluency can best be assessed by:
   a. Having the student retell or summarize the material to determine how much was understood.
   b. Giving a written test that covers plot, theme, character development, sequence of events, rising action, climax, falling action, and outcome. A student must test at a 95% accuracy rate to be considered fluent at silent reading.
   c. Giving a three-minute Test of Silent Contextual Reading Fluency four times a year. The student is presented with text in which spaces between words and all punctuation have been removed. The student must divide one word from another with slash marks, as in the following example: The/little/sailboat/bobbed/so/far/in/the/distance/it/looked/like/a/toy. The more words a student accurately separates, the higher her silent reading fluency score.
   d. Silent reading fluency cannot be assessed. It is a private act between the reader and the text and does not invite critique.

98. A high school teacher has given her students an assignment to write a non-rhyming poem of three lines. The first and last lines each contain five syllables, and the middle line contains seven syllables. The students are writing a:
   a. Limerick
   b. Metaphor
   c. Villanelle
   d. Haiku

99. "Verbal dyspraxia" refers to:
   a. Trouble with the physical act of writing.
   b. Confusing word or sentence order while speaking.
   c. Misplacement of letters within words.
   d. An inability to process verbal information.

100. "Coarticulation" affects:
   a. Blending awareness
   b. Phonemic awareness
   c. Sequencing
   d. Aural awareness

Answer Explanations

1. **A: Homophones.** Homophones are a type of homonym that sound alike, but are spelled differently and have different meanings. Other examples are *two, to,* and *too; their, they're,* and *there.*

2. **C: Argumentative essay.** The goal of a persuasive essay is to convince the reader that the author's position or opinion on a controversial topic is correct. That opinion or position is called the argument. A persuasive essay argues a series of points, supported by facts and evidence.

3. **D: Rate, accuracy, and prosody.** Fluent readers are able to read smoothly and comfortably at a steady pace (rate). The more quickly a child reads, the greater the chance of leaving out a word or substituting one word for another (for example, *sink* instead of *shrink*). Fluent readers are able to maintain accuracy without sacrificing rate. Fluent readers also stress important words in a text, group words into rhythmic phrases, and read with intonation (prosody).

4. **B: The number of unrecognizable words an English Language Learner encounters when reading a passage or listening to a teacher.** Language load is one of the barriers English Language Learners face. To lighten this load, a teacher can rephrase, eliminate unnecessary words, divide complex sentences into smaller units, and teach essential vocabulary before the student begins the lesson.

5. **A: A vowel.** A syllable is a minimal sound unit arranged around a vowel. For example, *academic* has four syllables: *a/ca/dem/ic.* It is possible for a syllable to be a single vowel, as in the above example. It is not possible for a syllable to be a single consonant.

6. **C: Fail, producing students at a Frustration reading level.** Those reading below grade level are likely to give up entirely. Those reading at grade level are likely to get frustrated and form habits that will actually slow down their development. Giving students texts that are too far beyond their reach produces frustrated readers. In an effort to succeed, frustrated writers are likely to apply strategies that have worked for them in the past but cannot work in this case because the text is simply beyond them. Looking for contextual clues to understand the meaning of unfamiliar words requires that most of the words in the passage are familiar. Breaking unfamiliar words into individual phonemes or syllables can be effective, but not if the number of such words is excessive. In this case, students below reading level and students at reading level will become frustrated when the skills that have worked for them in the past now fail.

7. **C: Tier-two words.** Tier-two words are words that are used with high frequency across a variety of disciplines or words with multiple meanings. They are characteristic of mature language users. Knowing these words is crucial to attaining an acceptable level of reading comprehension and communication skills.

8. **C: Reading at her Independent reading level.** When reading independently, students are at the correct level if they read with at least 97% accuracy.

9. B: To correct an error in reading a student has made, specifically clarifying where and how the error was made so that the student can avoid similar errors in the future. A reading teacher offers corrective feedback to a student in order to explain why a particular error in reading is, in fact, an error. Corrective feedback is specific; it locates where and how the student went astray so that similar errors can be avoided in future reading.

10. C: Content-specific words. Because these words are specific to paleontology, it's unlikely the students know their meanings. Without understanding what these words mean, the students would not be able to understand the content of the passage they were about to read.

11. B: Prior knowledge is knowledge the student brings from previous life or learning experiences to the act of reading. It is not possible for a student to fully comprehend new knowledge without first integrating it with prior knowledge. Prior knowledge, which rises from experience and previous learning, provides a framework by which new knowledge gained from the act of reading can be integrated. Every act of reading enriches a student's well of prior knowledge and increases that student's future ability to comprehend more fully any new knowledge acquired through reading.

12. B: Understanding of context and vocabulary. In a cloze test, a reader is given a text with certain words blocked out. The reader must be able to determine probable missing words based on contextual clues. In order to supply these words, the reader must already know them.

13. A: Common words with irregular spelling. Sight words occur in many types of writing; they are high-frequency words. Sight words are also words with irregular spelling. Some examples of sight words include *talk, some,* and *the.* Fluent readers need to recognize these words visually.

14. D: Consonant digraph. A consonant digraph is group of consonants in which all letters represent a single sound.

15. A: Phonological awareness. Phonemic awareness is the ability to recognize sounds within words. Segmenting words and blending sounds are components of phonemic awareness. Phonological awareness includes an understanding of multiple components of spoken language. Ability to hear individual words within a vocalized stream and ability to identify spoken syllables are types of phonological awareness.

16. A: Letter–sound correspondence. Letter–sound correspondence relies on the relationship between a spoken sound or group of sounds and the letters conventionally used in English to write them.

17. A: Strategy instruction. Strategic instruction involves teaching a methodic approach to solving a reading problem. It consists of strategies done in steps which aid the reader in eliminating incorrect responses.

18. D: Familiar, frequently used words that do not need to be taught beyond primary grades. Common or basic words are the first tier of three-tier words. These words are widely used across the spoken and written spectrum. Some examples are *walk, go, wish, the, look, happy,*

and *always.* This essential vocabulary is taught early in a reader's instruction, and beyond that it need not be taught.

19. B: The number of phonemes. A phoneme is the smallest measure of language sound. English language phonemes, about 40 in number, are composed of individual letters as well as letter combinations. A number of letters have more than one associated sound. For example, "c" can be pronounced as a hard "c" (cake) or a soft "c" (Cynthia). Vowels in particular have a number of possible pronunciations.

20. B: Consonant blend. Consonant blend refers to a group of consonants in which each letter represents a separate sound.

21. A: Fewer than 100 words in the time given. At the beginning of the school year, second-grade students should be able to read 50–80 words per minute. By the time they are well into the school year, second-grade-level reading is tracked at 85 words per minute.

22. D: None; sight words cannot be decoded. Readers must learn to recognize these words as wholes on sight. Sight words have irregular spelling. Segmenting them into syllables or using a phonemic approach are ineffective strategies to aid a reader in recognizing a sight word, because these approaches depend on rules a sight word doesn't follow. Word families group words that share common patterns of consonants and vowels. The spelling of those words is therefore regular, because they follow a predictable pattern. Sight words are irregular and do not follow a predictable pattern and must be instantaneously recognized for writing fluency. No decoding is useful.

23. D: A and B. English Language Learners are simultaneously learning to read in English and to apply patterns of intonation that are likely different from those of their first languages. While it's often useful to arrange reading time with a family member, in this particular case reading with a family member who is not a fluent English speaker may reinforce intonation patterns and pronunciation that are not correct. Therefore, C is not the answer. Both A and B afford English Language Learners the opportunity to become familiar with reading rates that are appropriate to the text and simultaneously expose them to prosody. They will not only see text, but will hear proper intonation patterns that are likely different than those of their first languages.

24. C: Alphabetic principle. The act of decoding involves first recognizing the sounds individual letters and letter groups make, and then blending the sounds to read the word. A child decoding the word *spin*, for example, would first pronounce *sp/i/n* as individual sound units. She then would repeat the sounds, smoothly blending them. Because decoding involves understanding letters and their sounds, it is sometimes known as the alphabetic principle.

25. C: Events. "Reading" a story's illustrations offers visual clues to characters and events in the proper order. A story's plot is what happens first, next, later, and finally.

26. A: Oral. Phonological awareness refers to an understanding of the sounds a word makes. While phonological awareness leads to fluent reading skills, activities designed to develop an awareness of word sounds are, by definition, oral.

27. B: Vocabulary. Strategizing in order to understand the meaning of a word, knowing multiple meanings of a single word, and applying background knowledge to glean a word's meaning are all ways in which an effective reader enhances vocabulary. Other skills include an awareness of word parts and word origins, the ability to apply word meanings in a variety of content areas, and a delight in learning the meanings of unfamiliar words.

28. C: She is reading at an Instructional level. In one minute, a student who misreads one or less than one word per twenty words, or with 95%–100% accuracy, is at an Independent reading level. A student who misreads one or less than one word per ten words, or with 90%–95% accuracy, is at an Instructional level. A student misreading more than one word out of ten, or with less than 90% accuracy, is at a Frustration level.

29. D: Decoding depends on an understanding of letter–sound relationships. As soon as a child understands enough letters and their correspondent sounds to read a few words, decoding should be introduced. The act of decoding involves first recognizing the sounds individual letters and letter groups in a word make and then blending the sounds to read the word. It's important to introduce the strategy as soon as a child knows enough letters and their corresponding sounds to read simple words.

30. C: Cause–effect words. Signal words give the reader hints about the purpose of a particular passage. Some signal words are concerned with comparing/contrasting, some with cause and effect, some with temporal sequencing, some with physical location, and some with a problem and its solution. The words *since, whether,* and *accordingly* are words used when describing an outcome. Outcomes have causes.

31. A: Outcome. Story action can be analyzed in terms of rising action, story climax, falling action, and resolution. Rising action consists of those events that occur before and lead up to the story's most dramatic moment, or climax. The climax occurs toward the end of the book, but rarely, if ever, right at the end. Following the climax, the consequences of that dramatic moment are termed falling action. The story reaches resolution with the outcome of the falling action.

32. C: Locate the vowels, then locate familiar word parts. Syllables are organized around vowels. In order to determine the syllables, this student should begin by locating the vowels. It's possible to have a syllable that is a single vowel (*a/gain*). It isn't possible to have a syllable that is a single consonant. Once the word has been broken into its component syllables the reader is able to study the syllables to find ones that are familiar and might give her a clue as to the word's meaning, such as certain prefixes or suffixes.

33. A: Nothing. These children are simply at an early stage in the reading/writing process. When emergent readers become aware of the connections between letters and sounds, and between reading and writing, they want to practice the skills they see proficient readers use. While a proficient writer knows that letters are grouped into words and that words are constructed into sentences that move from left to right and from the top of the page to the bottom, an emergent reader/writer knows only that letters magically contain sounds that other people can read. It is necessary for children to pass through early stages in which they scribble-write and pretend they are scripting letters, which leads to a stage in which they actually do write the initial letter of a word all over the page. Next, the emergent reader/writer will write the initial letter of many of the words that belong in the sentence and will write them sequentially. KJM, for example, might mean *the cat chased a mouse.*

34. A: Scripting the end-sound to a word (KT=cat); leaving space between words; writing from the top left to the top right of the page, and from top to bottom. Each of these steps is progressively more abstract. Scripting the end-sound to a word helps a young writer recognize that words have beginnings and endings. This naturally leads to the willingness to separate words with white space so that they stand as individual entities. Once this step is reached, the child realizes that in English, writing progresses from left to right and from the top of the page to the bottom.

35. B: Ask the students to read their stories to her. Suggest they visit other children in the class and read to each of them. The teacher should encourage these students by "reading" what they have written, even if what she reads is incorrect. She might misread KJM as *Kathy jumped rope with Mandy*. Most children will not be upset by this, but will correct the teacher's misreading by reading what the letters really mean.

36. D: The teacher should encourage all students to "read" picture books from the first day of school. Talking about the pictures from page to page gives young readers the idea that books are arranged sequentially. Pictures also offer narrative coherence and contextual clues. Emergent readers who are encouraged to enjoy books will more readily embrace the act of reading. Holding a book and turning pages gives young readers a familiarity with them.

37. D: Students should be taught that writing is a process. By teaching students to apply spelling patterns found in common phonemic units, the spelling of many words can be deduced. Sight words that are high frequency and do not follow patterns found in other words (*the, guardian, colonel*) must be taught.

38. C: Identify and use groups of letters that occur in a word family. Analogizing is based on recognizing the pattern of letters in words that share sound similarities. If the pattern is found at the end of a family of words, it is called a *rhyme*. Some examples of rhyme are *rent, sent, bent,* and *dent.* If the pattern is found at the beginning of the family of words, it is frequently a consonant *blend* such as *street, stripe,* or *strong,* in which all the letters are pronounced, or the pattern is a consonant digraph, in which the letters are taken together to represent a single sound such as in *phone, phonics,* or *phantom.*

39. A: Useful. The child will feel more confident because the story is already familiar. She will also feel that the lesson is a conversation of sorts, and that she is communicating successfully. She will be motivated to learn the English words because they are meaningful and highly charged. As a newly arrived immigrant, the child feels overwhelmed. Presenting her with a book of folk tales from her country tells her that she needn't lose her culture in order to function in this one. It also comforts her by reminding her that her past and present are linked. Allowing her to speak in Korean helps her express herself without fear of judgment or failure. Presenting her with an English vocabulary that is meaningful ensures that she will eagerly embrace these words, her first words in her new language.

40. D: Cultural load. Cultural load is concerned with how the relationship between language and culture can help or hinder learning. By using the Korean folk tale, the teacher offered the child the opportunity to learn new words in a context that was culturally familiar. By demonstrating respect for her student's culture, she helped lighten the cultural load.

41. C: Right and left; left. Researchers have discovered through brain imaging that a dyslexic reader uses both sides of the brain. Non-dyslexic readers use only the left side.

42. B: Revising. Revision (literally, re+vision) is the act of "seeing again." When revising, writers examine what they have written in order to improve the meaning of the work. Fine-tuning word choices, moving information to another location, and adding or deleting words are all acts of revision.

43. D: Prefixes, appearing at the beginning of base words to change their meanings. Suffixes appear at the end of words. Prefixes are attached to the beginning of words to change their meanings. *Un+happy, bi+monthly,* and *re+examine* are prefixes that, by definition, change the meanings of the words to which they are attached.

44. D: Dog, sit, leg. CVC words are composed of a consonant, a vowel, and a consonant. To learn to read them, students must be familiar with the letters used and their sounds. A teacher can present a word like *sit* to students who also know the consonants *b/f/h/p* and ask them to create a word family of other CVC words. The students will be able to read *bit, fit, hit,* and *pit* because they are similar to the word *sit* they have just learned.

45. C: Context. By considering the other words in the story, the student can determine the missing words. The student is depending on the information supplied by the rest of the story. This information puts the story into context.

46. D: All of the above. Metacognition means a reader's awareness of her own reading processes as she improves reading comprehension. Other elements of metacognition include awareness of areas in the text where the reader fails to comprehend and an understanding of how the text is structured.

47. A: Cooperative learning and reading comprehension. Cooperative learning occurs when a group of students at various levels of reading ability have goals in common. Reading comprehension is achieved through reading both orally and silently, developing vocabulary, a reader's ability to predict what will occur in a piece of writing, a reader's ability to summarize the main points in a piece of writing, and a reader's ability to reflect on the text's meaning and connect that meaning to another text or personal experience.

48. B: Understanding the meaning of words that are not familiar. Context cues offer insight into the probable meaning of unfamiliar words.

49. C: Observe the child over the course of a week or two. Draw her into conversation and determine if her vocabulary is limited, if she displays emotional problems, or if her reticence could have another cause. Note how the child interacts with others in the class. Does she ever initiate conversation? If another child initiates, does she respond? Until the teacher monitors the child's verbal abilities and habits, she cannot determine if the lack of interaction suggests a learning disability, an emotional problem, or simply a shy personality. The teacher should informally observe the child over a period of time, noting if and when she initiates or responds to oral language, if she is reading with apparent comprehension, if her vocabulary is limited, and the degree to which the child is interested in understanding.

50. B: Intervention. She can identify groups of letters, but is not able to apply letter–sound association. By first grade, a child should understand how to use word families to decode words. It is good that she can recognize the rhymes (common letter groups at the end of a word), but the fact that she does not know sounds associated with the letters that begin the word is troubling. She needs focused help on strengthening her ability to identify words.

51. C: Persuasive. The author is hoping to persuade or convince readers to avoid alcohol and tobacco by providing them with facts as well as by using rhetorical devices such as dispelling opposing arguments.

52. C: They meet to discuss areas the teacher is most concerned about and decide on the teacher's goals. In order to best achieve goals, those goals must be understood and established.

53. D: Being able to identify rhyme is an important element of phonological awareness. Young children use language in a solely oral way. Oral language is composed of separate sounds that are represented in written form by the alphabet. In order to read, a child must first have a sense of the sounds that are used in English (phonological awareness). By helping children hear the difference between rhyming and non-rhyming words, the teacher is preparing them to make the transition to sound–letter association and word families.

54. A: Closed, open, silent *e*, vowel team, vowel-*r*, and consonant-*le*. A closed syllable ends with a consonant, such as *cat*. Open syllables end with a vowel, such as *he*. Vowel team syllables contain two vowels working together, such as *main*. Vowel-*r* syllables such as *er* and *or* frequently occur as suffixes. Consonant-*le* syllables also typically occur as suffixes, such as *battle* or *terrible*.

55. A: Strategies to increase comprehension and to build vocabulary. The student should receive instruction focused on just those areas in which he is exhibiting difficulty. Improved vocabulary will give him greater skill at comprehending the meaning of a particular text. Strategies focused on enhancing comprehension together with a stronger vocabulary will provide the greatest help.

56. B: Through a combination of standardized testing, informal teacher observations, attention to grades, objective-linked assessments, and systematized charting of data over time. Reading comprehension and vocabulary cannot be sufficiently assessed with occasional, brief studies. Continuous observation, high-stakes and standardized testing, attention to grades, and closely tracking the outcomes of objective-linked assessments are interrelated tools that, when systematically organized, offer a thorough understanding of students' strengths and weaknesses.

57. A: An Oral Reading Fluency assessment. ORF stands for oral reading fluency. This assessment measures the words correct per minute (WCPM) by subtracting the number of errors made from the total number of words orally read in a one- to two-minute period of time. It is used to find a student's Instructional reading level, to identify readers who are having difficulties, and to track developing fluency and word recognition over time.

58. A: At the end of the year, to determine if instructional goals established at the beginning of the year have been successfully reached. An outcome assessment given at the end of the

year helps the reading teacher determine which students have reached instructional goals and do not need further support and which students will benefit from continued support.

59. D: Especially important to English Language Learners and students with reading disabilities. Word recognition is required for reading fluency and is important to all readers, but it is especially so to English Language Learners and students with reading disabilities. It can be effectively taught through precisely calibrated word study instruction designed to provide readers with reading and writing strategies for successful word analysis.

60. A: Proficiency with oral language enhances students' phonemic awareness and increases vocabulary. Understanding that words are scripted with specific letters representing specific sounds is essential to decoding a text. Students cannot effectively learn to read without the ability to decode. An enhanced vocabulary supports the act of reading; the larger an emergent reader's vocabulary, the more quickly he will learn to read. He will be able to decode more words, which he can organize into word families, which he can use to decode unfamiliar words.

61. The answer is c. Read the documents quickly, looking for key words in order to gather the basic premise of each. Skimming allows a reader to quickly gain a broad understanding of a piece of writing in order to determine if a more thorough reading is warranted. Skimming allows students who are researching a topic on the Internet or in print to consider a substantial body of information in order to select only that of particular relevance.

62. The answer is b. Expository. Expository essays clarify an idea, explain an event, or interpret facts. The position the author takes is often supported with statistics, quotations, or other evidence researched from a variety of sources.

63. B: Persuasive. A persuasive essay takes a strong position about a controversial topic and offers factual evidence to support this position. The goal of a persuasive paper is to convince the audience that the claim is true based on the evidence provided.

64. A: However, the myth of "safe cigarettes," questions about nicotine addiction, and denials about the dangers of secondhand smoke have proven to be propaganda and lies. A thesis statement offers a hypothesis or opinion that the remainder of the paper then sets out to prove. Oftentimes, the thesis statement also offers a clear road map of the paper, foreshadowing the focuses of the paragraphs that follow and the order in which they will appear.

65. The answer is d. The myth of "safe cigarettes," questions about nicotine addiction, and the dangers of secondhand smoke. These three foci are presented in the thesis statement in this order and will be fleshed out in the following three paragraphs as the body of the essay.

66. The answer is c. Example. Example essays, also called illustration essays, are simple, straightforward pieces that depend on clearly described examples to make their points. An example essay isn't trying to convince the reader (argumentative), compare similar or dissimilar things (compare/contrast), or point to relationships such as cause and effect. Often, example essays teach the reader how to accomplish something or about something.

67. C: Are homophones. Homophones are words that are pronounced the same, but differ in meaning. For example, a bride wears a 2 caret ring, but a horse eats a carrot.

68. A: Collaborative learning. A group of students working together on a project are applying numerous learning strategies at once. Collaborative learning is a hands-on approach that actively involves students in the learning process. Students involved in collaborative learning typically retain the lesson better.

69. C: Biography. A biography relates information about part of the life of an individual. An autobiography is a biography about the writer's own life. A memoir is also autobiographical, but focuses on a theme. Historical fiction uses a setting or event based in historical fact as the background for characters and/or action that is invented.

70. C: Students will do online research about the cultural, economic, or political events that were occurring during the specific time about which they've written. By researching the historic setting that cradled the events their interviewee discussed, students are simultaneously broadening their understanding of the context and working in a different content area.

71. B: Brainstorming and a compare/contrast strategy. Brainstorming is a prewriting activity in which an individual or group responds to a specific question by considering any and all responses that arise without editing, prioritizing, or selecting. Once the brainstorming session is complete, students look at the results and eliminate any responses that are not useful, then group and prioritize the remaining responses. In this example, the students are having a collaborative learning experience in that they are brainstorming together; however, collaborative learning is not a strategy per se, but is the outcome of a strategy. The students are also employing a compare/contrast strategy in that they are looking both at how the two writing styles share common elements and how they are distinct.

72. C: Writing styles. Both Anderson and the Grimms wrote in the same genre, that of fairy tales. Genre refers to types of writing. Mystery, romance, adventure, historical fiction, and fairy tales are some examples of genres. A genre can include many different authors and writing styles. These students are being asked to compare two distinct writing styles within a single genre in order to locate similarities and differences.

73. B: Comprehension. This exercise requires students to examine the authors' use of setting, plot, pacing, word choice, syntactical structures, narration, mood, metaphors, point of view, voice, and character development to find ways in which they are similar as well as different. In so doing, the students are discovering that language shapes meaning in ways both subtle and profound.

74. C: The importance of culture to meaning. Authors make thousands of decisions in the act of writing. What point of view to take, how much weight to give an event, what to reveal about a character, and what words will most effectively express the writer's intention are but a few of these decisions. While many of these decisions are consciously artistic choices, many are unconscious and imbedded in the cultural expectations of time and place in which the author has lived. To understand a text to the fullest degree possible, it is necessary to read it with an eye to the cultural framework from whence it came.

75. A: Give each child a piece of drawing paper that has been folded in half and then again, creating four boxes, along with a piece that has not been folded. The teacher should then ask the students to draw a cartoon about the story. Each of the first four boxes will show the events in order. The second page is to show how the story ends. When a child is able to visually see the way a familiar story has unfolded, that child can find causal or thematic connections in the action that increases her comprehension of the story overall. Asking the class to draw a single picture or to draw the beginning and end doesn't sufficiently demonstrate the importance of order to meaning. While some first graders may be able to create their own cartoon stories that demonstrate a logical series of events, many first graders are not yet ready to organize thought into a linear progression.

76. A: Sonnet. There are three primary types of sonnets. The Shakespearean sonnet is specifically what these students are reading. A Spenserian sonnet is also composed of three four-line stanzas followed by a two-line couplet; however, the rhymes are not contained within each stanza but spill from one stanza to the next (*abab bcbc cdcd ee*). A Petrarchan sonnet divides into an eight-line stanza and a six-line stanza.

77. D: Compare and contrast. Asking children to write a list provides them with a visual model that is a side-by-side comparison of the two countries. In creating that visual model, each student first has to organize his or her thoughts mentally, deciding whether each particular item under consideration shares more or less in common with the other.

78. C: *People celebrate marriages, births, and historical events.* The overlapping area is reserved for those items that are not culturally specific but are seen in both cultures.

79. D: A Venn diagram. A Venn diagram uses two or more circles with a common, overlapping area as a model to organize similar and dissimilar elements. The greater the number of similarities, the closer the circles must be and consequently, the greater the overlapping area. The fewer the number of similarities, the farther apart the circles will be and, consequently, the smaller the overlapping area.

80. A: Dysgraphia. Dysgraphic individuals have difficulty with the physical act of writing. They find holding and manipulating a pencil problematic. Their letters are primitively formed, and their handwriting is illegible.

81. B: Cliché. While "Pretty as a picture" is a simile (comparison of two unlike things using *like* or *as*), its overuse has turned it into a cliché. A cliché is a trite platitude.

82. B: Vocabulary. The tightly controlled syllabic requirements will cause students to search for words outside their normal vocabularies that will fit the rigid framework and still express the writer's intended meanings. Often, students will rediscover a word whose meaning they know, but they don't often use.

83. C: Brainstorming a list of verbs that mean ways of talking or ways of going, then adding them to the word wall along with some nouns that specify common topics. Second graders aren't developmentally ready for a thesaurus; most will believe that any words in a particular list are interchangeable. For example, a student who wrote *My little sister walks like a baby* might find the verbs *strut, sidle,* and *amble* in the thesaurus. None of these verbs would be an appropriate substitution. Supplementing a noun with an adjective often results in flat writing: *There's a tree in my yard* might become *There's a nice tree in my big yard.*

- 125 -

Adjectives such as *pretty, fun, cute, funny,* and so forth don't add much in terms of meaning, but they are the adjectives younger writers reach for first. A more specific noun is both more meaningful and more interesting. *There's a weeping willow in my yard* is evocative.

84. C: Explains to the parent that the child is not experiencing problems. She is correctly using the sight words she has learned, applying her knowledge of word families to determine spelling of similar words, and correctly hearing phonemes and scripting the words that represent them. Her strong verbal vocabulary and her reading skills are further evidence she is doing well. Her writing will catch up as she learns further strategies and sight words.

85. C: *Drip, chirp, splash, giggle.* Onomatopoeia refers to words that sound like what they represent.

86. D: It offers a systematic approach to untangling the wide variety of vowel sounds when an unfamiliar word is encountered. Code knowledge, also called orthographic tendencies, is a helpful approach to decoding a word when multiple pronunciation possibilities exist. For example, in the words *toe, go, though,* and *low,* the long O sound is written in a variety of ways. A code knowledge approach teaches a reader to first try a short vowel sound. If that doesn't help, the reader should consider the different ways the vowel or vowel groups can be pronounced, based on what he knows about other words.

87. D: Assess and target areas needing improvement as well as areas of greatest strength for each student to ensure the all members of a class are receiving instruction tailored to their specific needs.

88. A: Clarifying the goal, modeling strategies, and offering explanations geared to a student's level of understanding. Explicit instruction is well organized and structured, and it offers easily understood steps and depends in part on frequent reference to previously learned materials.

89. B: Scaffolding. Using this strategic approach, a teacher assigns a task that is just beyond the student's current level. The teacher encourages the student's attempts at comprehension by offering various supports that largely depend on prior knowledge, in order to develop the student's willingness to move forward into uncharted territory as a confident independent learner.

90. C: Write a compound word such as *doghouse* on the board. Underline *dog,* and then *house.* Beneath the words draw a picture of a dog and a house, joined with a plus sign. Next, write another compound word and ask the class to draw the pictures in their journals. Give the students a handout with several compound words. Ask them to underline the two words, then to draw the pictures. Students will discover that compound words are composed of two distinct words that in combination mean something new but related.

91. A: Reading comprehension. Prefixes and suffixes change the meanings of the root word to which they are attached. A student who understands that *un* means "not" will be able to decipher the meanings of words such as *unwanted, unhappy,* or *unreasonable.*

92. B: Closed syllables. Closed syllables are those that end with a consonant. *At, dog, spit, duck,* and *pluck* are all examples of closed syllables.

93. B: A maze test. A maze test is a specific type of cloze test. In a cloze test, words are deleted and the reader must supply the missing words using contextual clues and vocabulary that is familiar. A maze test is a multiple-choice application of a cloze test.

94. A: Avoid idioms and slang, involve students in hands-on activities, reference students' prior knowledge, and speak slowly. Teachers of English Language Learners should not employ idioms and slang in their instruction because these informal uses of speech are likely to confuse the students. Involving students in hands-on activities such as group reading and language play makes the experience both more meaningful and more immediate. New knowledge can only be absorbed by attaching it to prior knowledge, referencing what students already know is essential. Speaking slowly to English Language Learners is important, because they are processing what is being said at a slower rate than a native speaker.

95. A: Correcting surface features such as sentence fragments, spelling, and punctuation. Editing is the final step in the writing process. The writer has already decided the ideas or events are in proper order, have been sufficiently described, and are clear. Now the writer turns her attention to surface features, "scrubbing" errors in spelling, punctuation, and syntax from the writing.

96. A: Carefully organized lessons in decoding, sight words, vocabulary, and comprehension at least three to five times a week. These mini-lessons must be extremely clear, with the parts broken down to the lowest common denominator. The more tightly interwoven and systematized the instruction, the better chance this student will have. This type of learner needs, first and foremost, instruction that has been highly organized into a system that will make sense to her. If possible, she should receive private instruction on a daily basis. The instruction needs to focus on decoding, recognizing words, reading with increasing fluency, enhancing vocabulary, and comprehension. She should be working at the Instructional level, or with texts she can read with at least 90% accuracy.

97. C: Giving a three-minute Test of Silent Contextual Reading Fluency four times a year. The student is presented with text in which spaces between words and all punctuation have been removed. The student must divide one word from another with slash marks, as in the following example: *The/little/sailboat/bobbed/so/far/in/the/distance/it/looked/like/a/toy.* The more words a student accurately separates, then the higher her silent reading fluency score. Silent reading fluency can be monitored over time by giving the Test of Silent Contextual Reading Fluency (TSCRF) four times a year. A similar assessment tool is the Test of Silent Word Reading Fluency (TOSWRF), in which words of increasing complexity are given as a single, undifferentiated, and unpunctuated strand. As with the TSCRF, three minutes are given for the student to separate each word from the next. *Itwillcannotschoolbecomeagendaconsistentphilosophysuperfluous* is an example of such a strand.

98. D: Haiku. Based on a Japanese form of poetry, haiku have become popular with students and teachers alike. Reading and writing haiku helps younger students become aware of syllables and helps older students learn about subtleties of vocabulary.

99. B: Confusing word or sentence order while speaking. Dyspraxic individuals do not process spoken language sequentially due to a neurological distortion. The dislocation of

- 127 -

sounds within a word, such as vocalizing *lamp* instead of *palm*, is one indication of verbal dyspraxia.

100. B: Phonemic awareness. Vocalizing words involves arranging a series of continuous, voice, unvoiced, and stop sounds. As one sound is being uttered, the tongue and lips are already assuming the shape required by the next sound in the word. This process, which is not conscious, can distort individual sounds. One sound can slur into another, clip the end of the previous sound, or flatten or heighten a sound. For children who have difficulty hearing distinct phonemic sounds, individual instruction may be required.

Secret Key #1 - Time is Your Greatest Enemy

Pace Yourself

Wear a watch. At the beginning of the test, check the time (or start a chronometer on your watch to count the minutes), and check the time after every few questions to make sure you are "on schedule."

If you are forced to speed up, do it efficiently. Usually one or more answer choices can be eliminated without too much difficulty. Above all, don't panic. Don't speed up and just begin guessing at random choices. By pacing yourself, and continually monitoring your progress against your watch, you will always know exactly how far ahead or behind you are with your available time. If you find that you are one minute behind on the test, don't skip one question without spending any time on it, just to catch back up. Take 15 fewer seconds on the next four questions, and after four questions you'll have caught back up. Once you catch back up, you can continue working each problem at your normal pace.

Furthermore, don't dwell on the problems that you were rushed on. If a problem was taking up too much time and you made a hurried guess, it must be difficult. The difficult questions are the ones you are most likely to miss anyway, so it isn't a big loss. It is better to end with more time than you need than to run out of time.

Lastly, sometimes it is beneficial to slow down if you are constantly getting ahead of time. You are always more likely to catch a careless mistake by working more slowly than quickly, and among very high-scoring test takers (those who are likely to have lots of time left over), careless errors affect the score more than mastery of material.

Secret Key #2 - Guessing is not Guesswork

You probably know that guessing is a good idea - unlike other standardized tests, there is no penalty for getting a wrong answer. Even if you have no idea about a question, you still have a 20-25% chance of getting it right.

Most test takers do not understand the impact that proper guessing can have on their score. Unless you score extremely high, guessing will significantly contribute to your final score.

Monkeys Take the Test

What most test takers don't realize is that to insure that 20-25% chance, you have to guess randomly. If you put 20 monkeys in a room to take this test, assuming they answered once per question and behaved themselves, on average they would get 20-25% of the questions correct. Put 20 test takers in the room, and the average will be much lower among guessed questions. Why?

1. The test writers intentionally write deceptive answer choices that "look" right. A test taker has no idea about a question, so picks the "best looking" answer, which is often wrong. The monkey has no idea what looks good and what doesn't, so will consistently be lucky about 20-25% of the time.
2. Test takers will eliminate answer choices from the guessing pool based on a hunch or intuition. Simple but correct answers often get excluded, leaving a 0% chance of being correct. The monkey has no clue, and often gets lucky with the best choice.

This is why the process of elimination endorsed by most test courses is flawed and detrimental to your performance- test takers don't guess, they make an ignorant stab in the dark that is usually worse than random.

$5 Challenge

Let me introduce one of the most valuable ideas of this course- the $5 challenge:

You only mark your "best guess" if you are willing to bet $5 on it.

You only eliminate choices from guessing if you are willing to bet $5 on it.

Why $5? Five dollars is an amount of money that is small yet not insignificant, and can really add up fast (20 questions could cost you $100). Likewise, each answer choice on one question of the test will have a small impact on your overall score, but it can really add up to a lot of points in the end.

The process of elimination IS valuable. The following shows your chance of guessing it right:

If you eliminate wrong answer choices until only this many remain:	Chance of getting it correct:
1	100%
2	50%
3	33%

However, if you accidentally eliminate the right answer or go on a hunch for an incorrect answer, your chances drop dramatically: to 0%. By guessing among all the answer choices, you are GUARANTEED to have a shot at the right answer.
That's why the $5 test is so valuable- if you give up the advantage and safety of a pure guess, it had better be worth the risk.

What we still haven't covered is how to be sure that whatever guess you make is truly random. Here's the easiest way:

Always pick the first answer choice among those remaining.
Such a technique means that you have decided, **before you see a single test question**, exactly how you are going to guess- and since the order of choices tells you nothing about which one is correct, this guessing technique is perfectly random.

This section is not meant to scare you away from making educated guesses or eliminating choices- you just need to define when a choice is worth eliminating. The $5 test, along with a pre-defined random guessing strategy, is the best way to make sure you reap all of the benefits of guessing.

Secret Key #3 - Practice Smarter, Not Harder

Many test takers delay the test preparation process because they dread the awful amounts of practice time they think necessary to succeed on the test. We have refined an effective method that will take you only a fraction of the time.

There are a number of "obstacles" in your way to succeed. Among these are answering questions, finishing in time, and mastering test-taking strategies. All must be executed on the day of the test at peak performance, or your score will suffer. The test is a mental marathon that has a large impact on your future.

Just like a marathon runner, it is important to work your way up to the full challenge. So first you just worry about questions, and then time, and finally strategy:

Success Strategy

1. Find a good source for practice tests.
2. If you are willing to make a larger time investment, consider using more than one study guide- often the different approaches of multiple authors will help you "get" difficult concepts.
3. Take a practice test with no time constraints, with all study helps "open book." Take your time with questions and focus on applying strategies.
4. Take a practice test with time constraints, with all guides "open book."
5. Take a final practice test with no open material and time limits

If you have time to take more practice tests, just repeat step 5. By gradually exposing yourself to the full rigors of the test environment, you will condition your mind to the stress of test day and maximize your success.

Secret Key #4 - Prepare, Don't Procrastinate

Let me state an obvious fact: if you take the test three times, you will get three different scores. This is due to the way you feel on test day, the level of preparedness you have, and, despite the test writers' claims to the contrary, some tests WILL be easier for you than others.

Since your future depends so much on your score, you should maximize your chances of success. In order to maximize the likelihood of success, you've got to prepare in advance.

This means taking practice tests and spending time learning the information and test taking strategies you will need to succeed.

Never take the test as a "practice" test, expecting that you can just take it again if you need to. Feel free to take sample tests on your own, but when you go to take the official test, be prepared, be focused, and do your best the first time!

Secret Key #5 - Test Yourself

Everyone knows that time is money. There is no need to spend too much of your time or too little of your time preparing for the test. You should only spend as much of your precious time preparing as is necessary for you to get the score you need.

Once you have taken a practice test under real conditions of time constraints, then you will know if you are ready for the test or not.

If you have scored extremely high the first time that you take the practice test, then there is not much point in spending countless hours studying. You are already there.

Benchmark your abilities by retaking practice tests and seeing how much you have improved. Once you score high enough to guarantee success, then you are ready.

If you have scored well below where you need, then knuckle down and begin studying in earnest. Check your improvement regularly through the use of practice tests under real conditions. Above all, don't worry, panic, or give up. The key is perseverance!

Then, when you go to take the test, remain confident and remember how well you did on the practice tests. If you can score high enough on a practice test, then you can do the same on the real thing.

General Strategies

The most important thing you can do is to ignore your fears and jump into the test immediately- do not be overwhelmed by any strange-sounding terms. You have to jump into the test like jumping into a pool- all at once is the easiest way.

Make Predictions

As you read and understand the question, try to guess what the answer will be. Remember that several of the answer choices are wrong, and once you begin reading them, your mind will immediately become cluttered with answer choices designed to throw you off. Your mind is typically the most focused immediately after you have read the question and digested its contents. If you can, try to predict what the correct answer will be. You may be surprised at what you can predict.

Quickly scan the choices and see if your prediction is in the listed answer choices. If it is, then you can be quite confident that you have the right answer. It still won't hurt to check the other answer choices, but most of the time, you've got it!

Answer the Question

It may seem obvious to only pick answer choices that answer the question, but the test writers can create some excellent answer choices that are wrong. Don't pick an answer just because it sounds right, or you believe it to be true. It MUST answer the question. Once you've made your selection, always go back and check it against the question and make sure that you didn't misread the question, and the answer choice does answer the question posed.

Benchmark

After you read the first answer choice, decide if you think it sounds correct or not. If it doesn't, move on to the next answer choice. If it does, mentally mark that answer choice. This doesn't mean that you've definitely selected it as your answer choice, it just means that it's the best you've seen thus far. Go ahead and read the next choice. If the next choice is worse than the one you've already selected, keep going to the next answer choice. If the next choice is better than the choice you've already selected, mentally mark the new answer choice as your best guess.

The first answer choice that you select becomes your standard. Every other answer choice must be benchmarked against that standard. That choice is correct until proven otherwise by another answer choice beating it out. Once you've decided that no other answer choice seems as good, do one final check to ensure that your answer choice answers the question posed.

Valid Information

Don't discount any of the information provided in the question. Every piece of information may be necessary to determine the correct answer. None of the information in the question is there to throw you off (while the answer choices will certainly have information to throw you off). If two seemingly unrelated topics are discussed, don't ignore either. You can be confident there is a relationship, or it wouldn't be included in the question, and you are probably going to have to determine what is that relationship to find the answer.

Avoid "Fact Traps"

Don't get distracted by a choice that is factually true. Your search is for the answer that answers the question. Stay focused and don't fall for an answer that is true but incorrect. Always go back to the question and make sure you're choosing an answer that actually answers the question and is not just a true statement. An answer can be factually correct, but it MUST answer the question asked. Additionally, two answers can both be seemingly correct, so be sure to read all of the answer choices, and make sure that you get the one that BEST answers the question.

Milk the Question

Some of the questions may throw you completely off. They might deal with a subject you have not been exposed to, or one that you haven't reviewed in years. While your lack of knowledge about the subject will be a hindrance, the question itself can give you many clues that will help you find the correct answer. Read the question carefully and look for clues. Watch particularly for adjectives and nouns describing difficult terms or words that you don't recognize. Regardless of if you completely understand a word or not, replacing it with a synonym either provided or one you more familiar with may help you to understand what the questions are asking. Rather than wracking your mind about specific detailed information concerning a difficult term or word, try to use mental substitutes that are easier to understand.

The Trap of Familiarity

Don't just choose a word because you recognize it. On difficult questions, you may not recognize a number of words in the answer choices. The test writers don't put "make-believe" words on the test; so don't think that just because you only recognize all the words in one answer choice means that answer choice must be correct. If you only recognize words in one answer choice, then focus on that one. Is it correct? Try your best to determine if it is correct. If it is, that is great, but if it doesn't, eliminate it. Each word and answer choice you eliminate increases your chances of getting the question correct, even if you then have to guess among the unfamiliar choices.

Eliminate Answers

Eliminate choices as soon as you realize they are wrong. But be careful! Make sure you consider all of the possible answer choices. Just because one appears right, doesn't mean that the next one won't be even better! The test writers will usually put more than one good answer choice for every question, so read all of them. Don't worry if you are stuck between two that seem right. By getting down to just two remaining possible choices, your odds are now 50/50. Rather than wasting too much time, play the odds. You are guessing, but guessing wisely, because you've been able to knock out some of the answer choices that you know are wrong. If you are eliminating choices and realize that the last answer choice you are left with is also obviously wrong, don't panic. Start over and consider each choice again. There may easily be something that you missed the first time and will realize on the second pass.

Tough Questions

If you are stumped on a problem or it appears too hard or too difficult, don't waste time. Move on! Remember though, if you can quickly check for obviously incorrect answer choices, your chances of guessing correctly are greatly improved. Before you completely give up, at least try to knock out a couple of possible answers. Eliminate what you can and then guess at the remaining answer choices before moving on.

Brainstorm

If you get stuck on a difficult question, spend a few seconds quickly brainstorming. Run through the complete list of possible answer choices. Look at each choice and ask yourself, "Could this answer the question satisfactorily?" Go through each answer choice and consider it independently of the other. By systematically going through all possibilities, you may find something that you would otherwise overlook. Remember that when you get stuck, it's important to try to keep moving.

Read Carefully

Understand the problem. Read the question and answer choices carefully. Don't miss the question because you misread the terms. You have plenty of time to read each question thoroughly and make sure you understand what is being asked. Yet a happy medium must be attained, so don't waste too much time. You must read carefully, but efficiently.

Face Value

When in doubt, use common sense. Always accept the situation in the problem at face value. Don't read too much into it. These problems will not require you to make huge leaps of logic. The test writers aren't trying to throw you off with a cheap trick. If you have to go beyond creativity and make a leap of logic in order to have an answer choice answer the question, then you should look at the other answer choices. Don't overcomplicate the problem by creating theoretical relationships or explanations that will warp time or space. These are normal problems rooted in reality. It's just that the applicable relationship or explanation may not be readily apparent and you have to figure things out. Use your common sense to interpret anything that isn't clear.

Prefixes

If you're having trouble with a word in the question or answer choices, try dissecting it. Take advantage of every clue that the word might include. Prefixes and suffixes can be a huge help. Usually they allow you to determine a basic meaning. Pre- means before, post- means after, pro - is positive, de- is negative. From these prefixes and suffixes, you can get an idea of the general meaning of the word and try to put it into context. Beware though of any traps. Just because con is the opposite of pro, doesn't necessarily mean congress is the opposite of progress!

Hedge Phrases

Watch out for critical "hedge" phrases, such as likely, may, can, will often, sometimes, often, almost, mostly, usually, generally, rarely, sometimes. Question writers insert these hedge phrases to cover every possibility. Often an answer choice will be wrong simply because it leaves no room for exception. Avoid answer choices that have definitive words like "exactly," and "always".

Switchback Words

Stay alert for "switchbacks". These are the words and phrases frequently used to alert you to shifts in thought. The most common switchback word is "but". Others include although, however, nevertheless, on the other hand, even though, while, in spite of, despite, regardless of.

New Information

Correct answer choices will rarely have completely new information included. Answer choices typically are straightforward reflections of the material asked about and will directly relate to the question. If a new piece of information is included in an answer choice that doesn't even seem to relate to the topic being asked about, then that answer choice is likely incorrect. All of the information needed to answer the question is usually provided for you, and so you should not have to make guesses that are unsupported or choose answer choices that require unknown information that cannot be reasoned on its own.

Time Management

On technical questions, don't get lost on the technical terms. Don't spend too much time on any one question. If you don't know what a term means, then since you don't have a dictionary, odds are you aren't going to get much further. You should immediately recognize terms as whether or not you know them. If you don't, work with the other clues that you have, the other answer choices and terms provided, but don't waste too much time trying to figure out a difficult term.

Contextual Clues

Look for contextual clues. An answer can be right but not correct. The contextual clues will help you find the answer that is most right and is correct. Understand the context in which a phrase or statement is made. This will help you make important distinctions.

Don't Panic

Panicking will not answer any questions for you. Therefore, it isn't helpful. When you first see the question, if your mind goes blank, take a deep breath. Force yourself to mechanically go through the steps of solving the problem and using the strategies you've learned.

Pace Yourself

Don't get clock fever. It's easy to be overwhelmed when you're looking at a page full of questions, your mind is full of random thoughts and feeling confused, and the clock is ticking down faster than you would like. Calm down and maintain the pace that you have set for yourself. As long as you are on track by monitoring your pace, you are guaranteed to have enough time for yourself. When you get to the last few minutes of the test, it may seem like you won't have enough time left, but if you only have as many questions as you should have left at that point, then you're right on track!

Answer Selection

The best way to pick an answer choice is to eliminate all of those that are wrong, until only one is left and confirm that is the correct answer. Sometimes though, an answer choice may immediately look right. Be careful! Take a second to make sure that the other choices are not equally obvious. Don't make a hasty mistake. There are only two times that you should stop before checking other answers. First is when you are positive that the answer choice you have selected is correct. Second is when time is almost out and you have to make a quick guess!

Check Your Work

Since you will probably not know every term listed and the answer to every question, it is important that you get credit for the ones that you do know. Don't miss any questions through careless mistakes. If at all possible, try to take a second to look back over your answer selection and make sure you've selected the correct answer choice and haven't made a costly careless mistake (such as marking an answer choice that you didn't mean to mark). This quick double check should more than pay for itself in caught mistakes for the time it costs.

Beware of Directly Quoted Answers

Sometimes an answer choice will repeat word for word a portion of the question or reference section. However, beware of such exact duplication – it may be a trap! More than likely, the correct choice will paraphrase or summarize a point, rather than being exactly the same wording.

Slang

Scientific sounding answers are better than slang ones. An answer choice that begins "To compare the outcomes..." is much more likely to be correct than one that begins "Because some people insisted..."

Extreme Statements

Avoid wild answers that throw out highly controversial ideas that are proclaimed as established fact. An answer choice that states the "process should be used in certain situations, if…" is much more likely to be correct than one that states the "process should be discontinued completely." The first is a calm rational statement and doesn't even make a definitive, uncompromising stance, using a hedge word "if" to provide wiggle room, whereas the second choice is a radical idea and far more extreme.

Answer Choice Families

When you have two or more answer choices that are direct opposites or parallels, one of them is usually the correct answer. For instance, if one answer choice states "x increases" and another answer choice states "x decreases" or "y increases," then those two or three answer choices are very similar in construction and fall into the same family of answer choices. A family of answer choices is when two or three answer choices are very similar in construction, and yet often have a directly opposite meaning. Usually the correct answer choice will be in that family of answer choices. The "odd man out" or answer choice that doesn't seem to fit the parallel construction of the other answer choices is more likely to be incorrect.

Special Report: What is Test Anxiety and How to Overcome It?

The very nature of tests caters to some level of anxiety, nervousness or tension, just as we feel for any important event that occurs in our lives. A little bit of anxiety or nervousness can be a good thing. It helps us with motivation, and makes achievement just that much sweeter. However, too much anxiety can be a problem; especially if it hinders our ability to function and perform.

"Test anxiety," is the term that refers to the emotional reactions that some test-takers experience when faced with a test or exam. Having a fear of testing and exams is based upon a rational fear, since the test-taker's performance can shape the course of an academic career. Nevertheless, experiencing excessive fear of examinations will only interfere with the test-takers ability to perform, and his/her chances to be successful.

There are a large variety of causes that can contribute to the development and sensation of test anxiety. These include, but are not limited to lack of performance and worrying about issues surrounding the test.

Lack of Preparation

Lack of preparation can be identified by the following behaviors or situations:

- Not scheduling enough time to study, and therefore cramming the night before the test or exam
- Managing time poorly, to create the sensation that there is not enough time to do everything
- Failing to organize the text information in advance, so that the study material consists of the entire text and not simply the pertinent information
- Poor overall studying habits

Worrying, on the other hand, can be related to both the test taker, or many other factors around him/her that will be affected by the results of the test. These include worrying about:

- Previous performances on similar exams, or exams in general
- How friends and other students are achieving
- The negative consequences that will result from a poor grade or failure

There are three primary elements to test anxiety. Physical components, which involve the same typical bodily reactions as those to acute anxiety (to be discussed below). Emotional factors have to do with fear or panic. Mental or cognitive issues concerning attention spans and memory abilities.

Physical Signals

There are many different symptoms of test anxiety, and these are not limited to mental and emotional strain. Frequently there are a range of physical signals that will let a test taker know that he/she is suffering from test anxiety. These bodily changes can include the following:

- Perspiring
- Sweaty palms
- Wet, trembling hands
- Nausea
- Dry mouth
- A knot in the stomach
- Headache
- Faintness
- Muscle tension
- Aching shoulders, back and neck
- Rapid heart beat
- Feeling too hot/cold

To recognize the sensation of test anxiety, a test-taker should monitor him/herself for the following sensations:

- The physical distress symptoms as listed above
- Emotional sensitivity, expressing emotional feelings such as the need to cry or laugh too much, or a sensation of anger or helplessness
- A decreased ability to think, causing the test-taker to blank out or have racing thoughts that are hard to organize or control

Though most students will feel some level of anxiety when faced with a test or exam, the majority can cope with that anxiety and maintain it at a manageable level. However, those who cannot are faced with a very real and very serious condition, which can and should be controlled for the immeasurable benefit of this sufferer.

Naturally, these sensations lead to negative results for the testing experience. The most common effects of test anxiety have to do with nervousness and mental blocking.

Nervousness

Nervousness can appear in several different levels:

- The test-taker's difficulty, or even inability to read and understand the questions on the test
- The difficulty or inability to organize thoughts to a coherent form
- The difficulty or inability to recall key words and concepts relating to the testing questions (especially essays)

- The receipt of poor grades on a test, though the test material was well known by the test taker

Conversely, a person may also experience mental blocking, which involves:

- Blanking out on test questions
- Only remembering the correct answers to the questions when the test has already finished

Fortunately for test anxiety sufferers, beating these feelings, to a large degree, has to do with proper preparation. When a test taker has a feeling of preparedness, then anxiety will be dramatically lessened.

The first step to resolving anxiety issues is to distinguish which of the two types of anxiety are being suffered. If the anxiety is a direct result of a lack of preparation, this should be considered a normal reaction, and the anxiety level (as opposed to the test results) shouldn't be anything to worry about. However, if, when adequately prepared, the test-taker still panics, blanks out, or seems to overreact, this is not a fully rational reaction. While this can be considered normal too, there are many ways to combat and overcome these effects.

Remember that anxiety cannot be entirely eliminated, however, there are ways to minimize it, to make the anxiety easier to manage. Preparation is one of the best ways to minimize test anxiety. Therefore the following techniques are wise in order to best fight off any anxiety that may want to build.

To begin with, try to avoid cramming before a test, whenever it is possible. By trying to memorize an entire term's worth of information in one day, you'll be shocking your system, and not giving yourself a very good chance to absorb the information. This is an easy path to anxiety, so for those who suffer from test anxiety, cramming should not even be considered an option.

Instead of cramming, work throughout the semester to combine all of the material which is presented throughout the semester, and work on it gradually as the course goes by, making sure to master the main concepts first, leaving minor details for a week or so before the test.

To study for the upcoming exam, be sure to pose questions that may be on the examination, to gauge the ability to answer them by integrating the ideas from your texts, notes and lectures, as well as any supplementary readings.

If it is truly impossible to cover all of the information that was covered in that particular term, concentrate on the most important portions, that can be covered very well. Learn these concepts as best as possible, so that when the test comes, a goal can be made to use these concepts as presentations of your knowledge.

In addition to study habits, changes in attitude are critical to beating a struggle with test anxiety. In fact, an improvement of the perspective over the entire test-taking experience can actually help a test taker to enjoy studying and therefore improve the overall experience. Be certain not to overemphasize the significance of the grade - know that the result of the test is neither a reflection of self worth, nor is it a measure of intelligence; one grade will not predict a person's future success.

To improve an overall testing outlook, the following steps should be tried:

- Keeping in mind that the most reasonable expectation for taking a test is to expect to try to demonstrate as much of what you know as you possibly can.
- Reminding ourselves that a test is only one test; this is not the only one, and there will be others.
- The thought of thinking of oneself in an irrational, all-or-nothing term should be avoided at all costs.
- A reward should be designated for after the test, so there's something to look forward to. Whether it be going to a movie, going out to eat, or simply visiting friends, schedule it in advance, and do it no matter what result is expected on the exam

Test-takers should also keep in mind that the basics are some of the most important things, even beyond anti-anxiety techniques and studying. Never neglect the basic social, emotional and biological needs, in order to try to absorb information. In order to best achieve, these three factors must be held as just as important as the studying itself.

Study Steps

Remember the following important steps for studying:

- Maintain healthy nutrition and exercise habits. Continue both your recreational activities and social pass times. These both contribute to your physical and emotional well being.
- Be certain to get a good amount of sleep, especially the night before the test, because when you're overtired you are not able to perform to the best of your best ability.
- Keep the studying pace to a moderate level by taking breaks when they are needed, and varying the work whenever possible, to keep the mind fresh instead of getting bored.
- When enough studying has been done that all the material that can be learned has been learned, and the test taker is prepared for the test, stop studying and do something relaxing such as listening to music, watching a movie, or taking a warm bubble bath.

There are also many other techniques to minimize the uneasiness or apprehension that is experienced along with test anxiety before, during, or even after the examination. In fact, there are a great deal of things that can be done to stop anxiety from interfering with lifestyle and performance. Again, remember that anxiety will not be eliminated entirely, and it shouldn't be. Otherwise that "up" feeling for exams would not exist, and most of us depend on that sensation to perform better than usual. However, this anxiety has to be at a level that is manageable.

Of course, as we have just discussed, being prepared for the exam is half the battle right away. Attending all classes, finding out what knowledge will be expected on the exam, and knowing the exam schedules are easy steps to lowering anxiety. Keeping up with work will remove the need to cram, and efficient study habits will eliminate wasted time. Studying should be done in an ideal location for concentration, so that it is simple to become interested in the material and give it complete attention. A method such as SQ3R (Survey, Question, Read, Recite, Review) is a wonderful key to follow to make sure that the study habits are as effective as possible, especially in the case of learning from a textbook. Flashcards are great techniques for memorization. Learning to take good notes will mean that notes will be full of useful information, so that less sifting will need to be done to seek out what is pertinent for studying. Reviewing notes after class and then again on occasion will keep the information fresh in the mind. From notes that have been taken summary sheets and outlines can be made for simpler reviewing.

A study group can also be a very motivational and helpful place to study, as there will be a sharing of ideas, all of the minds can work together, to make sure that everyone understands, and the studying will be made more interesting because it will be a social occasion.

Basically, though, as long as the test-taker remains organized and self confident, with efficient study habits, less time will need to be spent studying, and higher grades will be achieved.

To become self confident, there are many useful steps. The first of these is "self talk." It has been shown through extensive research, that self-talk for students who suffer from test anxiety, should be well monitored, in order to make sure that it contributes to self confidence as opposed to sinking the student. Frequently the self talk of test-anxious students is negative or self-defeating, thinking that everyone else is smarter and faster, that they always mess up, and that if they don't do well, they'll fail the entire course. It is important to decreasing anxiety that awareness is made of self talk. Try writing any negative self thoughts and then disputing them with a positive statement instead. Begin self-encouragement as though it was a friend speaking. Repeat positive statements to help reprogram the mind to believing in successes instead of failures.

Helpful Techniques

Other extremely helpful techniques include:

- Self-visualization of doing well and reaching goals
- While aiming for an "A" level of understanding, don't try to "overprotect" by setting your expectations lower. This will only convince the mind to stop studying in order to meet the lower expectations.
- Don't make comparisons with the results or habits of other students. These are individual factors, and different things work for different people, causing different results.
- Strive to become an expert in learning what works well, and what can be done in order to improve. Consider collecting this data in a journal.

- Create rewards for after studying instead of doing things before studying that will only turn into avoidance behaviors.
- Make a practice of relaxing - by using methods such as progressive relaxation, self-hypnosis, guided imagery, etc - in order to make relaxation an automatic sensation.
- Work on creating a state of relaxed concentration so that concentrating will take on the focus of the mind, so that none will be wasted on worrying.
- Take good care of the physical self by eating well and getting enough sleep.
- Plan in time for exercise and stick to this plan.

Beyond these techniques, there are other methods to be used before, during and after the test that will help the test-taker perform well in addition to overcoming anxiety.

Before the exam comes the academic preparation. This involves establishing a study schedule and beginning at least one week before the actual date of the test. By doing this, the anxiety of not having enough time to study for the test will be automatically eliminated. Moreover, this will make the studying a much more effective experience, ensuring that the learning will be an easier process. This relieves much undue pressure on the test-taker.

Summary sheets, note cards, and flash cards with the main concepts and examples of these main concepts should be prepared in advance of the actual studying time. A topic should never be eliminated from this process. By omitting a topic because it isn't expected to be on the test is only setting up the test-taker for anxiety should it actually appear on the exam. Utilize the course syllabus for laying out the topics that should be studied. Carefully go over the notes that were made in class, paying special attention to any of the issues that the professor took special care to emphasize while lecturing in class. In the textbooks, use the chapter review, or if possible, the chapter tests, to begin your review.

It may even be possible to ask the instructor what information will be covered on the exam, or what the format of the exam will be (for example, multiple choice, essay, free form, true-false). Additionally, see if it is possible to find out how many questions will be on the test. If a review sheet or sample test has been offered by the professor, make good use of it, above anything else, for the preparation for the test. Another great resource for getting to know the examination is reviewing tests from previous semesters. Use these tests to review, and aim to achieve a 100% score on each of the possible topics. With a few exceptions, the goal that you set for yourself is the highest one that you will reach.

Take all of the questions that were assigned as homework, and rework them to any other possible course material. The more problems reworked, the more skill and confidence will form as a result. When forming the solution to a problem, write out each of the steps. Don't simply do head work. By doing as many steps on paper as possible, much clarification and therefore confidence will be formed. Do this with as many homework problems as possible, before checking the answers. By checking the answer after each problem, a reinforcement will exist, that will not be on the exam. Study situations should be as exam-like as possible, to prime the test-taker's system for the experience. By waiting to check the answers at the end, a psychological advantage will be formed, to decrease the stress factor.

Another fantastic reason for not cramming is the avoidance of confusion in concepts, especially when it comes to mathematics. 8-10 hours of study will become one hundred percent more effective if it is spread out over a week or at least several days, instead of doing it all in one sitting. Recognize that the human brain requires time in order to assimilate new material, so frequent breaks and a span of study time over several days will be much more beneficial.

Additionally, don't study right up until the point of the exam. Studying should stop a minimum of one hour before the exam begins. This allows the brain to rest and put things in their proper order. This will also provide the time to become as relaxed as possible when going into the examination room. The test-taker will also have time to eat well and eat sensibly. Know that the brain needs food as much as the rest of the body. With enough food and enough sleep, as well as a relaxed attitude, the body and the mind are primed for success.

Avoid any anxious classmates who are talking about the exam. These students only spread anxiety, and are not worth sharing the anxious sentimentalities.

Before the test also involves creating a positive attitude, so mental preparation should also be a point of concentration. There are many keys to creating a positive attitude. Should fears become rushing in, make a visualization of taking the exam, doing well, and seeing an A written on the paper. Write out a list of affirmations that will bring a feeling of confidence, such as "I am doing well in my English class," "I studied well and know my material," "I enjoy this class." Even if the affirmations aren't believed at first, it sends a positive message to the subconscious which will result in an alteration of the overall belief system, which is the system that creates reality.

If a sensation of panic begins, work with the fear and imagine the very worst! Work through the entire scenario of not passing the test, failing the entire course, and dropping out of school, followed by not getting a job, and pushing a shopping cart through the dark alley where you'll live. This will place things into perspective! Then, practice deep breathing and create a visualization of the opposite situation - achieving an "A" on the exam, passing the entire course, receiving the degree at a graduation ceremony.

On the day of the test, there are many things to be done to ensure the best results, as well as the most calm outlook. The following stages are suggested in order to maximize test-taking potential:

- Begin the examination day with a moderate breakfast, and avoid any coffee or beverages with caffeine if the test taker is prone to jitters. Even people who are used to managing caffeine can feel jittery or light-headed when it is taken on a test day.

- Attempt to do something that is relaxing before the examination begins. As last minute cramming clouds the mastering of overall concepts, it is better to use this time to create a calming outlook.
- Be certain to arrive at the test location well in advance, in order to provide time to select a location that is away from doors, windows and other distractions, as well as giving enough time to relax before the test begins.
- Keep away from anxiety generating classmates who will upset the sensation of stability and relaxation that is being attempted before the exam.
- Should the waiting period before the exam begins cause anxiety, create a self-distraction by reading a light magazine or something else that is relaxing and simple.
- During the exam itself, read the entire exam from beginning to end, and find out how much time should be allotted to each individual problem. Once writing the exam, should more time be taken for a problem, it should be abandoned, in order to begin another problem. If there is time at the end, the unfinished problem can always be returned to and completed.

Read the instructions very carefully - twice - so that unpleasant surprises won't follow during or after the exam has ended.

When writing the exam, pretend that the situation is actually simply the completion of homework within a library, or at home. This will assist in forming a relaxed atmosphere, and will allow the brain extra focus for the complex thinking function.

Begin the exam with all of the questions with which the most confidence is felt. This will build the confidence level regarding the entire exam and will begin a quality momentum. This will also create encouragement for trying the problems where uncertainty resides.

Going with the "gut instinct" is always the way to go when solving a problem. Second guessing should be avoided at all costs. Have confidence in the ability to do well.

For essay questions, create an outline in advance that will keep the mind organized and make certain that all of the points are remembered. For multiple choice, read every answer, even if the correct one has been spotted - a better one may exist.

Continue at a pace that is reasonable and not rushed, in order to be able to work carefully. Provide enough time to go over the answers at the end, to check for small errors that can be corrected.

Should a feeling of panic begin, breathe deeply, and think of the feeling of the body releasing sand through its pores. Visualize a calm, peaceful place, and include all of the sights, sounds and sensations of this image. Continue the deep breathing, and take a few minutes to continue this with closed eyes. When all is well again, return to the test.

If a "blanking" occurs for a certain question, skip it and move on to the next question. There will be time to return to the other question later. Get everything done that can be done, first, to guarantee all the grades that can be compiled, and to build all of the confidence possible. Then return to the weaker questions to build the marks from there.

Remember, one's own reality can be created, so as long as the belief is there, success will follow. And remember: anxiety can happen later, right now, there's an exam to be written!

After the examination is complete, whether there is a feeling for a good grade or a bad grade, don't dwell on the exam, and be certain to follow through on the reward that was promised...and enjoy it! Don't dwell on any mistakes that have been made, as there is nothing that can be done at this point anyway.

Additionally, don't begin to study for the next test right away. Do something relaxing for a while, and let the mind relax and prepare itself to begin absorbing information again. From the results of the exam - both the grade and the entire experience, be certain to learn from what has gone on. Perfect studying habits and work some more on confidence in order to make the next examination experience even better than the last one.

Learn to avoid places where openings occurred for laziness, procrastination and day dreaming.

Use the time between this exam and the next one to better learn to relax, even learning to relax on cue, so that any anxiety can be controlled during the next exam. Learn how to relax the body. Slouch in your chair if that helps. Tighten and then relax all of the different muscle groups, one group at a time, beginning with the feet and then working all the way up to the neck and face. This will ultimately relax the muscles more than they were to begin with. Learn how to breathe deeply and comfortably, and focus on this breathing going in and out as a relaxing thought. With every exhale, repeat the word "relax."

As common as test anxiety is, it is very possible to overcome it. Make yourself one of the test-takers who overcome this frustrating hindrance.

Special Report: Retaking the Test: What Are Your Chances at Improving Your Score?

After going through the experience of taking a major test, many test takers feel that once is enough. The test usually comes during a period of transition in the test taker's life, and taking the test is only one of a series of important events. With so many distractions and conflicting recommendations, it may be difficult for a test taker to rationally determine whether or not he should retake the test after viewing his scores.

The importance of the test usually only adds to the burden of the retake decision. However, don't be swayed by emotion. There a few simple questions that you can ask yourself to guide you as you try to determine whether a retake would improve your score:

1. What went wrong? Why wasn't your score what you expected?

- Can you point to a single factor or problem that you feel caused the low score? Were you sick on test day? Was there an emotional upheaval in your life that caused a distraction? Were you late for the test or not able to use the full time allotment? If you can point to any of these specific, individual problems, then a retake should definitely be considered.

2. Is there enough time to improve?

- Many problems that may show up in your score report may take a lot of time for improvement. A deficiency in a particular math skill may require weeks or months of tutoring and studying to improve. If you have enough time to improve an identified weakness, then a retake should definitely be considered.

3. How will additional scores be used? Will a score average, highest score, or most recent score be used?

- Different test scores may be handled completely differently. If you've taken the test multiple times, sometimes your highest score is used, sometimes your average score is computed and used, and sometimes your most recent score is used. Make sure you understand what method will be used to evaluate your scores, and use that to help you determine whether a retake should be considered.

4. Are my practice test scores significantly higher than my actual test score?

- If you have taken a lot of practice tests and are consistently scoring at a much higher level than your actual test score, then you should consider a retake. However, if you've taken five practice tests and only one of your scores was higher than your actual test score, or if your practice test scores were only slightly higher than your actual test score, then it is unlikely that you will significantly increase your score.

5. Do I need perfect scores or will I be able to live with this score? Will this score still allow me to follow my dreams?

- What kind of score is acceptable to you? Is your current score "good enough?" Do you have to have a certain score in order to pursue the future of your dreams? If you won't be happy with your current score, and there's no way that you could live with it, then you should consider a retake. However, don't get your hopes up. If you are looking for significant improvement, that may or may not be possible. But if you won't be happy otherwise, it is at least worth the effort.
- Remember that there are other considerations. To achieve your dream, it is likely that your grades may also be taken into account. A great test score is usually not the only thing necessary to succeed. Make sure that you aren't overemphasizing the importance of a high test score.
- Furthermore, a retake does not always result in a higher score. Some test takers will score lower on a retake, rather than higher. One study shows that one-fourth of test takers will achieve a significant improvement in test score, while one-sixth of test takers will actually show a decrease. While this shows that most test takers will improve, the majority will only improve their scores a little and a retake may not be worth the test taker's effort.
- Finally, if a test is taken only once and is considered in the added context of good grades on the part of a test taker, the person reviewing the grades and scores may be tempted to assume that the test taker just had a bad day while taking the test, and may discount the low test score in favor of the high grades. But if the test is retaken and the scores are approximately the same, then the validity of the low scores are only confirmed. Therefore, a retake could actually hurt a test taker by definitely bracketing a test taker's score ability to a limited range.

Special Report: Additional Bonus Material

Due to our efforts to try to keep this book to a manageable length, we've created a link that will give you access to all of your additional bonus material.

Please visit http://www.mometrix.com/bonus948/priireadspec to access the information.